1981

1. The Grand Teton, Snake River; Storm. The subject values were deep and somber. Reflections of the sky in the water are of Zone VII-VIII values in the print. (Direct reflection of the sun would fall on Zone XI and above. The contrast of the subject is expanded in the negative, and the original print shows maximum range of tones from black to white.)

THE PRINT

CONTACT PRINTING AND ENLARGING

ANSEL ADAMS

Basic Photo 3

NEW YORK GRAPHIC SOCIETY • BOSTON

The photographer who combines scientific method with artistic skill is in the best possible position to do good work.

Hurter and Driffield
(*Photo-Miniature*, No. 56, 1903)

I extend my appreciation and thanks to my friends and associates who have helped so generously in the preparation of this book. Among them are Miss Lee Benedict, Miss Charlotte Mauk, and Mr. P. B. Knight. The diagrams and the book design are by Milton Cavagnaro.

I dedicate these books to everyone who is interested in the development of straightforward photography and who believes in the simple statement of the lens.

International Standard Book Number: 0-8212-0718-0
Library of Congress Catalog Card Number: 76-50536

HOR
New York Graphic Society books are published by Little, Brown and Company. Published simultaneously in Canada by Little, Brown and Company (Canada) Limited

Printed in the United States of America

iv

FOREWORD

The function of this series, *Basic Photo*, is to present a philosophy of technique and application. Every example and statement is set forth with the hope that the photographer and the serious student will use it as the basis for personal experiment and for the development of a personal approach.

Photography, in the final analysis, can be reduced to a few simple principles. But, unlike most arts, it seems complex at the initial approach. The seeming complexity can never be resolved unless a fundamental understanding of both technique and application is sought and exercised from the start.

Photography is more than a medium for factual communication of ideas. It is a creative art. Therefore emphasis on technique is justified only so far as it will simplify and clarify the statement of the photographer's concept. These books are intended to present essential ideas and to suggest applications of photographic methods to practical problems of artistic expression. Our object is to present a working technique for creative photography.

Certain controls whereby the photographer may achieve desired qualities in his negative are discussed in Book 2 (*The Negative*). Book 3 is devoted to printing and enlarging and discusses essential controls applied to this final step in expressive photography. It also includes sections on equipment, darkroom, materials, toning, mounting, formulas, and detailed expositions of procedure.

Visualization (Book 2, page 21) includes all steps from the selection of the subject to the final print; the negative is but one essential step in the complete process and the finished print is the final step. A finished print cannot be technically evaluated without consideration of the original visualization, the exposure and development of the negative, and the mechanical and esthetic possibilities of the printing process. Thus Books 2 and 3 are not truly separable, as none of the three chief factors of my approach to photography—visualization, the negative, and the print—has any true significance by itself. Visualization of the final print should dominate the making of the negative, which is only a means to an end, and of the print, which is the expressive statement, but which is susceptible to interpretative controls and modifications that broaden or intensify the original concept of the photograph.

We may draw an analogy with music: The composer entertains a musical idea. He sets it down in conventional musical notation. When he performs it, he may, although respecting the score, inject personal expressive interpretations on the basic patterns of the notes. So it is in expressive photography: The concept of the photograph precedes the operation of the camera. Exposure and development of the negative follow technical patterns selected to achieve the qualities desired in the final print, and the print itself is somewhat of an interpretation, a performance of the photographic idea.

Hence I feel that although certain precise mechanistic controls are of the utmost importance in making a negative, there should be a minimum of rigid mechanical control in making a print. A purely expressive approach can be used if the original creative concept is clear and the photographer has adequate technical ability. I see no reason why any control that is of purely photographic nature is not valid. However, I believe that the border line of good taste usually lies this side of retouching or employment of texture screens, diffusion and distortion devices, paper negatives, and methods such as bromoil and gum printing, all of which, in my opinion, deviate from strictly "straight" photographic procedure.

Present-day materials are, in the main, of superb quality, flexibility, and simplicity. The entire photographic process of today, from exposure and development of the negative through contact printing or enlarging, is of maximum directness and simplicity. It is the mastery of this direct and effective process with which we are concerned in this and other books of the *Basic Photo Series*.

It must be clearly understood by everyone that the philosophy and approach set forth in this book are definitely those of Ansel Adams, and while of course there is no deviation from basic principles, terminology and the inclusion of expressive factors may differ in some instances from conventional photographic terminology and practical procedure. It is my firm conviction that a useful bridge between sensitometry and the more scientific aspects of the medium, and practical creative work, has never been adequately constructed. This book sets forth a working procedure based on my personal methods—as expressed in my own photography and in my teaching. I ask of my readers a degree of attention consistent with serious study, and I also urgently suggest that the testing and general procedures be fully carried out so that the photographer may grasp the full significance of visualization and planned execution in creative photography.

2. Sunlight on Old Boards. Negative exposed for average brightness value of boards placed on Zone V, and given normal-plus-plus development. Print was made on Velour Black Glossy No. 2 paper, developed in Beers No. 4. A slight degree of toning in selenium augments the effect of brilliancy in the original print. Blacks are solid and crisp; whites show texture.

TABLE OF CONTENTS

FOREWORD v

THE EXPRESSIVE PRINT 1

PRINTING PROCESSES: A HISTORICAL NOTE 2

PHOTOGRAPHIC PAPERS 4

PROPERTIES OF PHOTOGRAPHIC PAPERS 9

THE DARKROOM 27

PROCESSING THE PRINT 45

DETAILED DESCRIPTION OF MAKING A PRINT 60

DETAILED DESCRIPTION OF MAKING AN ENLARGEMENT 73

PROBLEMS OF CONTROL 75

DETAILED DESCRIPTION OF TONING 78

MOUNTING 83

ETCHING AND SPOTTING OF PRINTS 91

MAKING PRINTS FOR REPRODUCTION 95

MASS PRODUCTION OF PRINTS 99

PHOTO MURALS, OVERMANTELS, SCREENS 104

FORMULAS 112

INDEX 119

Illustrations

1. THE GRAND TETON, SNAKE RIVER; STORM ii
2. SUNLIGHT ON OLD BOARDS vi
3. OLD DOORWAY, NEW JERSEY viii
4. SYMBOLIC CURVES (EXAGGERATED) 7
5. SYMBOLIC CURVES FOR PAPERS OF DIFFERENT CONTRAST GRADES 10
6. NEW CHURCH, TAOS PUEBLO, NEW MEXICO 11
7. THE WESTON STEP-WEDGE 13
8. DEVELOPING CURVES FOR A CHLORIDE PAPER 15
9. DEVELOPING CURVES FOR A BROMIDE PAPER 15
10. FARM, MOUNT DIABLO RANGE, CALIFORNIA 16
11. HEAD OF NISEI GIRL, MANZANAR, CALIFORNIA 20
12. NEVADA FALL, YOSEMITE VALLEY 26
13. THE GRAND CANYON, ARIZONA 30
14. SCHEMATIC DIAGRAM OF CONTACT-PRINTING ASSEMBLY 32
15. LEAF PATTERN 33
16. SCHEMATIC DIAGRAM OF A HORIZONTAL ENLARGER ASSEMBLY 35
17. BOULDER DAM (HOOVER DAM), CALIFORNIA 38
18. SCHEMATIC DIAGRAM OF ENLARGER ILLUMINATION 41
19. COLONIAL DOORWAY, NEW JERSEY 44
20. WINERY INTERIOR, LODI, CALIFORNIA 48
21. CHURCH, SAN FRANCISCO 51
22. NEW YORK CITY 52
23. EFFECTS OF WATER-BATH AND STATIC DEVELOPMENT 53
24. AUTUMN, GLACIER NATIONAL PARK, MONTANA 59
25. ILLUSTRATING A TYPICAL TEST PRINT 63
26. GOLDEN GATE BRIDGE 66
27. DEMONSTRATIONS OF EDGE-BURNING 67
28. ILLUSTRATING DODGING EFFECTS 68
29. ILLUSTRATING POOR DODGING AND BURNING 69
30. SYMBOLIC DODGING AND BURNING SYMBOLS 70
31. TIOGA LAKE, EXAGGERATED EFFECT OF BURNING 71
32. HALF DOME, WINTER, YOSEMITE VALLEY. WITH GRAY SCALE 72
33. PORTRAIT: MAYNARD DIXON, TUCSON, ARIZONA 77
34. SAN FRANCISCO RESIDENCE 81
35. WOOD AND ROCK, NOON SUN, SIERRA NEVADA 82
36. PLACEMENT OF PRINTS OF VARIOUS PROPORTIONS ON MOUNTS 85
37. SCHEMATIC DIAGRAMS OF METHODS OF ATTACHING DRY-MOUNTING TISSUE TO THE BACKS OF PRINTS 87
38. SCHEMATIC DIAGRAMS: DRY-MOUNTING PRESS ASSEMBLY 89
39. THE WATCH TOWER, MESA VERDE NATIONAL PARK, COLORADO 90
40. GAS STATION, CHEMURGIC COMPANY PLANT, RICHMOND, CALIFORNIA 95
41. THE WHITE CHURCH, HORNITOS, CALIFORNIA 98
42. PORTRAIT, PRIEST AT MARIPOSA, CALIFORNIA 102
43. SCREEN: ORCHARD IN WINTER 107
44. SCHEMATIC DIAGRAM: CROSS SECTION OF A LARGE PRINT BEING PROCESSED 109

3. Old Doorway, New Jersey. The effect of brilliancy and texture is derived from juxtaposition of minute areas of white and black against a general average of neutral gray values. The reproduction cannot convey the intensity of the extreme blacks or the pure whites.

THE EXPRESSIVE PRINT

I assume that the reader's interest lies in the production of expressive photographs—not mere factual representations. Hence the techniques of both negative and print must be under imaginative control at all times. I also assume that the reader has thoroughly acquainted himself with the material presented in Book 2 of this series (*The Negative*); if he has not done so, the approach and the terminology of this book may be slightly confusing.

We should know what we desire in our print before we expose the negative. Then we expose and develop the negative to achieve the required sequence of opacities that is the foundation of the visualized print or enlargement. But we must remember that the print need not be a literal transcription of the negative any more than the negative is a literal transcription of the values in the subject photographed. And the print, of course, cannot be a literal transcription of the subject.

The selection of paper surface is a matter of individual choice. Both Edward Weston and I prefer unferrotyped glossy surfaces; Paul Strand chooses semigloss surfaces of fine texture; Alfred Stieglitz employed a variety of papers. To assume that the use of glossy paper assures success is indeed a fallacy; in fact, the revealing nature of glossy surfaces merely exaggerates inadequacies of concept and technique. My choice of paper surface is dictated by the desire to achieve images of maximum clarity and brilliancy with a minimum suggestion of paper texture. But for specific problems I may select other surfaces, a high-gloss print for a small but especially brilliant image (such as a 4x5 snow scene), or a semigloss, slightly textured paper for a photomural or a photo screen (in which the paper texture actually augments the impression of definition in the greatly enlarged image and makes the inevitable spotting a simpler task). After spotting, such papers may be waxed, varnished, or sprayed with a colorless protective plastic.

From a negative in which the opacities bear a reasonable relation to the reflectances (brilliancies) * in the visualized print, prints of many subtle variations of tonalities can be made. Although the actual difference of values in various prints made from the same negative may be rather small, the emotional effect of such slight variations may be considerable. As a rule, I have found that the most expressive prints are usually of somewhat deeper tonality than a literal transcription of the negative (or of the subject) would suggest. The printing procedure outlined on page 60 may represent only the first stages of making a print. On examination of the first print, even after it is mounted and spotted, the photographer may become acutely aware of the need for some variation of effect to express his concept more intensely, or to expand his original concept. His next print may depart considerably from his original intent. Elastic and fluid attitudes of thought and feeling should dominate both the original concept and the making of the print. In the planning and making of any expressive print we must remember that it is the image itself, not a mere arbitrary sequence of tonal values, which conveys the photographer's concept.

---

* Refer to the description of terms in Book 2, p. vi.

PRINTING PROCESSES: A HISTORICAL NOTE*

The first negative and positive photographs were produced on paper impregnated with silver salts. These calotype negatives often showed great richness of values with an almost complete absence of halation. Delicate detail, however, was obscured by the texture of the paper base. While today many pictorialists make intermediate paper negatives because this destruction of detail gives effects considered "artistic" by them, and because the negative can easily be retouched, early photographers were dissatisfied. In an attempt to match the exquisite perfection of the daguerreotype they tried to eliminate the texture of the paper support by waxing it, but still they had to put up with broad effects. The negatives were printed on uncoated silver-chloride paper that darkened visibly during exposure.

Strictly speaking, daguerreotypes are neither negatives nor positives: the shadows are brilliantly polished silver areas and the highlights are whitish silver amalgam. Only when the shadows reflect a dark field does the daguerreotype appear to be a positive. The delicate beauty of the daguerreotype and the relative simplicity of its technique made the process immensely popular, and it was the most widely used photographic medium well into the 1850's. In the daguerreotype the microscopic revelation of the lens was fully expressed. I confess that I frequently appraise my work by critical comparison with the daguerreotype image; how urgently I desire to achieve that exquisite tonality and miraculous definition of light and substance in my own prints!

In 1851 both the calotype and the daguerreotype became obsolescent with the introduction of the collodion or wet-plate process, which made it possible to use glass as a negative support. To reproduce the fine detail recorded by these negatives, paper was coated with egg white to give it a smooth, even surface. This albumen paper gave a visible image on exposure to daylight. It was toned in gold chloride, fixed, washed, and burnished with hot steel rollers. At the end of the century collodion and gelatin took the place of albumen. These silver printing-out papers (P.O.P.) could give results of great richness. But too often they were impermanent.

Substitute processes were therefore invented that made no use of silver. The carbon process relies upon the property of potassium bichromate to render gelatin insoluble in water on exposure to light. A pigment—usually powdered carbon —is mixed with the bichromatized gelatin. After exposure the print is "developed" in warm water, which washes away the unexposed, and consequently still soluble, gelatin. The technique is exacting, for it is necessary to transfer the pigmented gelatin to a fresh surface during processing. Another drawback is the difficulty of judging exposure time, since the image becomes visible only after processing. Were it not so time-consuming, it might be more extensively used, because the image is detailed and of long scale, the surface is smooth, and the tone can be precisely determined by choice of appropriate pigment.

A variation, the carbro or ozobrome process, is somewhat simpler. A bromide print is placed in contact with carbon tissue treated with potassium ferricyanide, which reacts with the silver image in such a way that the gelatin is insolubilized.

---

* For a more detailed discussion, see Beaumont Newhall, *The History of Photography from 1839 to the Present Day*, New York, The Museum of Modern Art, 1949; and L. P. Clerc, *Theory and Practice of Photography*, London, 1947. I am indebted to Mr. Newhall for his kind assistance in compiling this short historical chapter.

Processing is similar to that of carbon prints, with the advantage that the result is more predictable. The gum process depends on the relative solubility of bichromatized gum arabic mixed with a pigment. In hot water the gum can be completely dissolved, and in the 1890's, when pictorialists deliberately imitated drawings, gum prints were popular because unwanted details could be washed away.

Platinum salts produce prints of superior lasting quality, but it was rather for esthetic reasons that the platinotype process was so widely used in the closing years of the last century. It did not necessitate coating the paper, with the consequence that soft prints with the texture of the paper support could be secured. Iron salts made the paper light-sensitive and precipitated finely divided platinum during processing. The palladiotype, which makes use of less expensive salts of palladium, was worked in the same fashion. Both processes weathered the stylistic change in photographic esthetics that came about in the 1920's; the paper was either waxed to disguise its texture, or supplied doubly coated on smooth stock.

All these papers gradually fell into disuse with the growth of gelatinobromide developing-out papers or D.O.P., so called because exposure gave a latent image that was developed in a fashion similar to that used on dry plates or film. D.O.P. had the advantage that the photographer no longer must rely on the sun. The first types introduced in the 1880's were called "gaslight papers"; they were printed with the gas on full and developed with the gas turned low. A further reason for their popularity was that the manufacturer could furnish paper in differing grades of contrast. The need for this came about with the introduction of roll film, which precluded individual development of each negative; photographers were taught that there was an optimum development time for each combination of film, developing agent, and temperature. The craft of developing negatives to fit a certain paper gave way to the choice of a paper to fit an automatically produced negative. However, as the reader of my earlier books is aware, I believe that success in photography necessitates a technique that will permit one to produce on paper an image visualized in all its detail before the camera shutter is opened. In place of the craft methods of the past I advocate the rational use of controls that science has taught us. To produce negatives to fit a specific type of paper is a return to the traditions of photography.

A Short List of Helpful Books on Photography

Hill, David Octavius, and Adamson, Robert: Schwarz, Heinrich, *David Octavius Hill, Master of Photography*, New York, 1931

Emerson, Peter Henry: *Naturalistic Photography*, London, 1889; 1898

Carrol, John S.: *Photo-Lab-Index* 23rd ed., New York, 1964

Morgan, Willard D.: *The Leica Manual*, 14th ed., New York 1963
       Graphic-Graflex Photography, 11th ed., New York, 1958

Atget, Eugene: *Atget, Photographe de Paris*, New York, 1930

Stieglitz, Alfred: *Stieglitz Memorial Portfolio*, ed. by Dorothy Norman, New York, 1947

Strand, Paul: Newhall, Nancy, *Paul Strand*, New York, 1945

Weston, Edward: *Fifty Photographs by Edward Weston*, New York, 1946

Adams, Ansel: *Making a Photograph*, rev. ed., London, 1949
       My Camera in Yosemite Valley, Boston and Yosemite, 1949
       My Camera in the National Parks, Boston and Yosemite, 1950
       Polaroid Land Photography Manual, New York, 1963

PHOTOGRAPHIC PAPERS

Although most modern photographs are printed on developing-out papers, several types of printing-out paper are still in use, and the photographer should investigate their possibilities. The most common use of printing-out papers is for portrait proofs. However, when properly handled, printing-out papers can be used to make expressive prints of extraordinary beauty and tonal range.*

If one were to attempt to print on modern papers from old wet-plate negatives, such as Brady's plates of the Civil War, he would realize that the characteristics of present-day negatives and papers are vastly different from those of earlier times. Many of these old plates are of almost incredible harshness. I once had serious difficulty making adequate prints from an early set, although using the softest obtainable contact and projection papers, and Amidol developer diluted to from 1/10 to 1/15 of the normal concentration. Even at that, the qualities of the negatives were not fully revealed; their opacity range vastly exceeded the exposure range of the softest modern paper.

The reason for the apparent long scale of printing-out papers is not any inherent flexibility in the emulsion itself, but rather a progressive self-masking process. As light strikes these printing-out emulsions, the silver halides are directly reduced to metallic silver, and the silver in the image then acts as a screen to the light. The denser the image, the less light can penetrate the depths of the emulsion, and consequently the less the effect of prolonged exposure on already darkened areas. A very contrasty negative printed on P.O.P. yields an image of extraordinary range of values; extending exposure beyond that required to give good value in the dark portions of the print has relatively little additional effect on these parts of the image, but may reveal astonishing subtleties in the near-whites and light grays.

Of course it should be clearly understood that the maximum brilliancy (reflection density) range of any photographic print is limited; printing-out papers will not give a print image of greater brilliancy range than developing-out papers of the same surface and having the same maximum deposit of silver. But they will *interpret* a negative of much greater opacity range, and the tones and colors in a well-processed P.O.P. image are usually rich enough to further intensify the impression of long tonal scale and brilliancy.

The image on a printing-out paper is made permanent by treatment in toning and fixing baths, which are quite different, however, from those used with developing-out papers. Formulas are given on page 117.

For those interested in the *photogram*—semi- or pseudo-abstract designs produced by shadows, reflections, or direct applications of light to the sensitive paper and not employing images produced by the lens (except with "montage" combinations)—the printing-out papers offer great possibilities. With these papers the designs can be seen in their various stages from the start; with developing-out papers the results are revealed only on completion of development. Sunlight or strong artificial light may be used as desired.

---

* Some printing-out paper processes are described in such reference works as Neblette's *Photography, Its Principles and Practice,* or *Handbook of Photography* by Henney and Dudley, or in manuals published before the turn of the century.

The modern developing-out papers may be grouped into three general divisions:

First is the *contact-printing type, in* which the emulsion is composed chiefly of silver chloride. These papers are mostly relatively slow, but have a good scale and fine tonal values. They are used for direct contact printing from the negative, being usually too slow for enlarging purposes except when extremely powerful lights are used. Typical brands of contact-printing paper are Apex, Azo, Convira, and Velox. These are often scorned as being mere "commercial papers," but it should be remembered that some of the finest modern prints have been made on them. Attest the major part of Stieglitz's or Weston's work. As is shown later (page 33), it is entirely possible to make contact prints on enlarging papers, if suitable lights are used. Varigam (page 8) can easily be used for either contact printing or enlarging; different grades of contrast are achieved by the use of special filters.

The next division includes the *chlorobromide or bromochloride* papers, the name depending on whether silver bromide or silver chloride is preponderant in the emulsion. These are moderately fast enlarging papers, but may also be used for contact printing under weak light. They have considerable richness of tone and are usually amenable to slight direct toning in metallic salts—selenium, for example. Typical brands of such papers are Cykora, Illustrators' Special, Koda-bromide, and Velour Black.

In the third type of developing-out papers, called *bromide* papers, the emulsion is made up almost entirely of silver bromide. With the exception of some types for special uses, such as Kodaline Bromide and Solar Bromide, they are the fastest of all photographic papers, approaching in speed and characteristics the slower negative emulsions. Their use is chiefly limited to enlarging. Typical examples of such papers are Brovira, Halobrom, and Royal Bromide. Their speed is of the order of 1000 times that of average contact-printing paper, and they must be handled almost as carefully as slow negative material, so far as darkroom illumination is concerned. Some workers argue that bromide papers do not yield so rich a tonal scale as chloride and chlorobromide papers, but I feel that this is more a matter of the limitations of certain brands and a lack in the processor's ability than a question of the shortcomings of bromide papers in general. Some of my finest prints have been produced on fast bromide papers, not only by enlarging, but also by contact printing with weak amber light.*

Owing to the relatively large grain structure of the bromide-paper emulsion, direct metallic toners, such as selenium, have little effect on it, but bromide papers may be toned by the redevelopment-sulfide process, the hypo-alum, Nelson gold-toning, tellurium, and other processes (see page 57).

We should not overlook the positive transparency, either single or stereoscopic images, as these have astonishing brilliancy and emotional impact. The lantern slide is the most familiar form of this somewhat neglected field.

---

* Except for Varigam (page 8) most photographic papers are sensitive only to blue light (some bromide papers have a slight red sensitivity as well). The ordinary amber lamp passes some blue light; we may therefore say that the paper can be affected by the residual blue light from a presumably safe amber lamp.

Photographic papers, being designed for various purposes, are given qualities appropriate to certain practical and emotional requirements. Such qualities may be tangible or intangible. Among the tangible qualities are:

1. *Surface texture and brilliance.* When we look at a print we see a silver image in terms of reflected light. The maximum practical brilliancy is attained on a smooth, glossy surface, and amounts to a range of about 1 to 50 (possibly, as an extreme, 1 to 60). A rough matte surface has the lowest brilliancy—perhaps no more than 1 to 15 or 1 to 20. Between these extremes lie many combinations of sheen and texture. The principal forms are designated glossy, semigloss, semimatte, matte, rough, etc.; many surfaces, however, bear names given them by the manufacturer (such as Velvet, Silk, Porcelain Stipple, Kashmir); or they are designated more simply by a combination of numbers or letters (such as Kodabromide F, and Velour Black S).

2. *Color of stock.* Photographic papers are made in a fairly wide range of colors: Cold White (white with a slightly bluish cast), Natural White (white with a very slight ivory cast), Ivory White, Cream, and Buff. There seems to be no standard of color designation in use by the various manufacturers, so that it is difficult to describe accurately any particular paper.

The total effect of the image is influenced not only by qualities 1 and 2, but also by print color.

3. *Print color.* This is a property of both emulsion and paper base, and is modified by the development, and still further modified by toning (see page 57). Some paper emulsions are basically "cold-toned," some are "warm-toned," and there are many steps between. Convira, for instance, is listed as having a cold, blue-black tone, Cykora, as yielding a warm tone. Developer formulas are designed to favor warm or cold tones; the warmest tones are naturally obtained by using a warm-tone developer on a warm-tone paper.

The tones and colors that have become more or less standard in photography are seldom attractive to me, in themselves. I know of no modern paper on which the superb tones of platinum or carbon images can be even approached without careful selection of developer and subsequent toning. The olive-green-black of many "warm-toned" papers does not, in my opinion, enhance the brilliance and richness of the silver image. It is of the greatest importance that definite standards of color be established for both print and paper—just as we have accepted standards for paints, fabrics, and other materials. As it is, photographers are confused by the uncertain application of casual terminology.

4. *Body or weight.* We have a choice of "single-weight" or "double-weight," and occasionally even of "middle-weight" and "lightweight" stock—but again, what do such designations imply? Single-weight papers are practical when the prints are small or are to be dried on belt driers. Double-weight papers withstand the rigors of processing much better than single-weight sheets, being less subject to ridging and breaking (see page 56); although they are not as practical to dry on ferrotype plates, they lie much flatter after drying on cloth frames or on blotters, and can be mounted with greater ease and with smoother results (see page 83). My personal preference is for double-weight paper, and I use it for practically every purpose, including big enlargements for murals, screens, and display, although single-weight papers are usually recommended for that purpose.

I have found that in processing and mounting large sheets of single-weight stock it is practically impossible to avoid some physical damage. Thorough washing of a large sheet of paper requires considerable handling—rolling and moving about —and single-weight stock is certain to suffer thereby. (See page 109 for discussion of the problems of washing large prints).

I list as the intangible qualities:

5. *Contrast.* The exposure range or contrast in a print suggests the response of the paper to the light transmitted through the negative. The exposure range of the paper should be suited to the opacity range of the negative in order that all its values may be fully revealed in the print. A negative viewed by transmitted light may reveal an opacity range of 1 to 10, 1 to 100, or even 1 to 1000 or more; but a print seen by reflected light has a maximum brilliancy range of about 1 to 50. We must remember this fundamental difference; the opacity range of the negative is not in itself of esthetic importance, but the brilliancy range of a print is definitely of great importance. In other words, a print should exhibit a complete range of tones, as well as the extremes—white and black—in order to have strength and conviction. The amounts of pure white and solid black may be very small, but in almost every case, either one or both of these extremes should appear in order to "key" the values. The subtleties of a very deep gray or of a delicately textured white may be lost unless there be some solid black or pure white to make clear their proper place on the tonal scale.

6. *Tonal scale.* Two papers having the same exposure scale may produce prints of different quality. Although the limits of the tonal scale may be the same, the progression of values *within* the scale is determined by those properties of the paper which are expressed in its characteristic curve (see Book 2). If the curve has a fairly long toe, the whites are more subtly rendered than in a paper whose

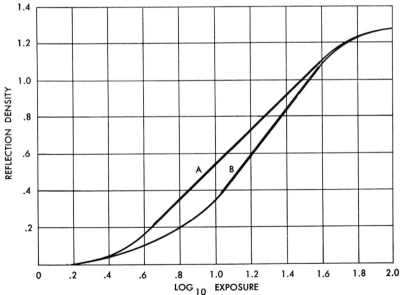

4. Symbolic Curves (exaggerated). A represents "commercial" paper; B represents "portrait" paper. Both papers have the same total exposure scale, but B shows a more lenient progression of values in the toe of the curve (giving more variation in the whites of the image).

curve has a more abrupt toe, and in which whites are compacted so that the transition from white to darker values of the scale is more abrupt. "Portrait" papers are usually of the former type, "commercial" papers of the latter. See Figure 4, page 7.

While some papers are more expensive than others, the standard brands of developing-out papers fall, in my opinion, within a very reasonable price range. In relation to the time involved in making fine prints, and the basic cost of darkroom and equipment, the cost of the paper itself is negligible.

As the technical aspects of photography are often overemphasized, we may be inhibited in our expressive work by a too-critical attitude toward the physical subtleties of the various printing papers. Granted that some papers are better than others, not only intrinsically but in direct relation to the individual's work, it is nevertheless a fact that most differences—short of obviously defective manufacture —can in many cases be overcome by an intelligent appraisal of the properties of the paper, and the necessary adjustments in exposing and developing procedures required for the desired effects. Testing for the exposure scale of the paper (pages 11-12) will reveal many of its properties.

Summing up my personal preferences in photographic papers and printing procedures: I use commercial-type emulsions—such as Kodabromide and Velour Black—for most of my work, stressing the double-weight, cold-white stock, and the glossy (but unferrotyped) surface. I work for a cool purple-black image by using a cold-toned developer and a slight toning in selenium. With this combination, I feel that I achieve an image of maximum strength and beauty of print color—an image that is logically related to the clean crisp sharpness of the image formed by the lens.

Varigam

There is no need to describe here the technique of printing with DuPont Varigam, as full operating instructions accompany packages of this product. Suffice to say that when used with special filters over the printing or enlarging lights, this paper yields a variety of contrasts (10 grades in all). It is important that the proper safelights and printing filters — and of course the proper color of printing and enlarging lights — be used; otherwise the procedures of testing and printing on Varigam are quite similar to that described in this book for regular papers, except that the desired contrasts are achieved on one grade of paper by using various filters, rather than by selecting different grades of paper to match the negative. The quality of the prints is excellent; the paper has most of the attributes of Velour Black. Kodak Polycontrast is an excellent variable contrast paper.

The question I raise about this paper does not relate to its physical qualities which are very fine indeed. Rather I feel that the extreme flexibility of contrast control that not only permits use of a wide variety of negatives, but also makes possible various contrasts from different parts of the same negative in a single print, may encourage the photographer to be less careful about his negatives. Continued carelessness in visualization and controlled exposure and development (even if it could always be fully corrected in the physical sense by this flexible printing process) would shortly dull the perceptive abilities. Too much would be left to fortune and too little to serious creative intention. On the other hand, if the extended controls offered by Varigam are fully understood and appreciated when the photograph is first visualized, there is no reason why this relatively new product cannot be of great value to the photographer.

PROPERTIES OF PHOTOGRAPHIC PAPERS

Exposure Scales

Just as with negative emulsions (Book 2), printing and enlarging paper emulsions have definite curves of response to exposure. As a rule, paper curves are much more abrupt; the greater the contrast of the paper, the steeper its characteristic curve.

Our chief concern is with the total effective scale of the paper, from a faint tone below the white of the paper base to the densest obtainable black, and with how many units of exposure are necessary to encompass this entire range.

Exposure scales represent the required number of units of exposure of the print emulsion to produce maximum black if one unit of exposure is defined as that producing the first perceptible step of tone below the white of the paper stock.

If, for example, a paper requires an exposure of 1 second (with a light of given intensity) to produce a tone just perceptibly darker than that of the paper base, and 25 seconds' exposure to produce the maximum black of which the paper is capable (with a standard developer and under normal viewing conditions), we may say that this paper has an exposure scale of 1 to 25, or 25; expressed in logarithms, the designation would be 1.40. Now if the opacity range of the negative were 1 to 25 (negative density 1.40), this paper would record all the values in the negative from the deepest blacks to the lightest tones. In other words, we would have a full-scale print encompassing all the values in the negative. However, the print does not necessarily have to encompass the entire range of opacities in the negative. Since the effective exposure scale of the paper is referred not to white but to the faintest perceptible tone below the white of the paper base, any opacity in the negative that prints pure white lies outside the range that must be related to the effective exposure scale of the paper. We need not be concerned with trying to compress the actual (perhaps extreme) range of opacities in a negative into a scale suitable for a given paper, so long as the *significant* tonalities can be suitably expressed in the print. Image values visualized as pure white should obviously be printed as pure white, and must be represented in the negative as suitably high opacities. See Figure 5, page 10.

Most published exposure scales for papers exclude the extreme ends of the scale (the limits of the toe and the shoulder of the characteristic curve), as these extremes are not considered within the "useful" response of the paper emulsion. Actually, the subtleties of the lightest and darkest tones involve the entire range of the paper's sensitivity; in fact, it has been my experience that qualities characterizing a truly fine print may be found in the delicate values of the extremely light and dark portions.

There is a most unfortunate confusion in regard to paper grades, whether indicated by number or by other terms, and this confusion is aggravated by the manufacturers' exposure-scale ratings for various papers. For instance, "No. 2 paper" is a most casual designation; this grade number represents quite different exposure scales in the products of various manufacturers. Even among the products of one manufacturer, the contrast-grade indications for different types of paper are not alike. Furthermore, the characteristics of various papers may be dissimilar, some having a longer toe to their curve than others, and such qualities are difficult to convey in a single designation.

9

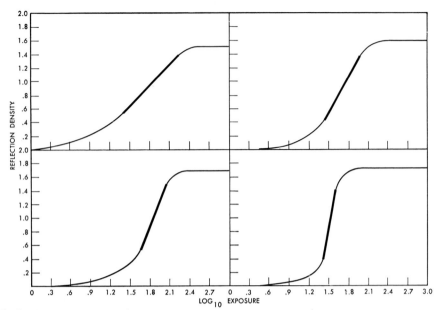

5. Symbolic Curves for Papers of Different Contrast Grades. Steepness of the straight-line section indicates exposure scale of the paper. The steepest curve represents the shortest scale, hence that grade of paper would be used for negatives of lowest contrast. Note that the effective total density of each grade is somewhat alike, but the exposure scales vary from about 1.7 (50) to about 0.7 (5). The curves relate to no particular paper brand; they are simply a graphic representation of differences in contrast grades.

Since the clear gelatin-emulsion coating on a photographic paper has a slight density, the whitest area of the print is never quite so white as the paper stock would be without the gelatin coating. In some papers, the baryta coating (the clay coating on the paper stock) is intentionally less brilliant than the paper stock. This is supposed to improve press-reproduction qualities.

Testing for Effective Exposure Scale

The response of any print paper, hence its effective exposure scale varies with the developer used. Just what may be expected of a given paper under given conditions may be determined with the aid of a step wedge and the Weston Fotoval. See figure 7, page 13 and text, page 12.

A negative step wedge is essentially a negative divided into a series of small areas ranging from low to high density. It can be calibrated by the use of a densitometer (such as the Kodak Color Densitometer, or the Weston Fotoval). A print made from it reveals the extremes of densities to which the paper responds, according to its exposure scale. A series of tests in which identically exposed prints are carefully processed in various developers will show how the effective exposure scale can be influenced by choice of a developer.

Results of an actual test with the Beers and Kodak D-72 formulas (page 113) are seen in the table on page 12. The figures represent one particular test; with a different brand of paper (or even another batch of the same paper), with a different light, or with a different developer, the results could be quite different. (I do not list the results for all seven of the possible Beers mixtures; the norm and

6. New Church, Taos Pueblo, New Mexico. Brilliancy in the print image is obtained partially by textural effects and the juxtaposition of very dark and very light values—not by image contrast only. The illusion of light is very important. While a softer print might reveal more definition in the shadows, the allover effect of bright cold light would be lost.

the extremes are represented by mixtures number 1, number 4, and number 7, and it is easy to infer what effects the other mixtures would have.) It is important to recognize that a test of this type does not define the paper in sensitometric terms; that would require exact exposures and carefully controlled development beyond the facilities—or the needs—of the practicing photographer. This particular test does emphasize, however, the wide range of control possible with various combinations of the Beers two-solution developer.

The Weston step wedge I used for this test has a density range of 0.04 to 1.80. I made prints from it and analyzed them by determining which step in the negative corresponded to the first visually perceptible tone below pure white in the print and which step gave as dark a tone as was to be found in the print; the *difference* between the densities of those steps represented the effective exposure scale of the paper *with the developer used.*

It should be noted that it is quite possible (if the exposure is short) to obtain pure white in the print from something less than the maximum density in a normal negative; however, if the exposure is adjusted so that—with this wedge— step No. 20 remains white and No. 19 shows the first perceptible tone, then there will be a greater range of lower tones to work with.

The step-by-step procedure for the test is as follows:

1. Select paper; adjust printing lights; prepare developer, stop bath, and fixing bath.

2. Make a fog test as follows:
    a. Mix the Beers stock solutions without bromide or antifoggant.
    b. Prepare the desired working solution (No. 4, No. 7, or whatever).
    c. Add a small quantity of potassium-bromide solution (see formula, page 118), or other restrainer (try 25 cc of .4% benzotriazole) per liter of working solution.
    d. Place a piece of unexposed paper in the developer and agitate it constantly. Be certain that the safelight is shielded. If the paper fogs within 5 minutes, add a little more of the antifoggant—but not more than is required to prevent fog within 5 minutes' development time. Using more may result in higher contrast than is normally required.
3. Make a test exposure and develop for 2 minutes. Several trial exposures may be necessary before the proper exposure time to show the first trace of tone in wedge No. 19 is determined.
4. Make an actual print from the step-wedge negative, measuring accurately the proper exposure time.
5. Fix, wash, and dry as usual. Evaluate the print only when dry.

If another Beers mixture is used, it may be necessary to retest for proper exposure to get the desired value for No. 19.

TEST FOR EFFECTIVE EXPOSURE RANGE OF A PAPER WITH DIFFERENT DEVELOPERS

Data for this test: Kodabromide No. 2. Weston Step Wedge (calibrated at factory). Printing light: mercury-argon in diffusion enlarger. (The intensity of such lights varies from the norm for a few seconds after switching on.)

Method of printing: In printing frame placed on enlarger easel. (Step wedge in printing frame, not in the enlarger.)

Timing of exposure: Electric metronome, set at 100.

Method of exposure: By withdrawing and replacing card at lens. Enlarging light burning constantly.

Developer	*Density Range of Step Wedge Calculated from Step 1 below Pure White to Maximum Black*	*Effective Exposure Scale in Arithmetic Units*
D 72 1:2	1.50	32
BEERS 1 1:1	1.76	58
BEERS 1 —	1.70	50
BEERS 4	1.50	32
BEERS 7	1.34	22
With Kodabromide No. 1		
BEERS 7	1.50	32
With Kodabromide No. 3		
BEERS 1	1.55	35

Note that with Beers 7, the exposure scale of Kodabromide No. 1 is the same as with Kodabromide No. 2 and Beers 4. Note that with Beers 1, the exposure scale of Kodabromide No. 3 is approximately the same as with Kodabromide No. 2 and Beers 4.

ENLARGING TESTS: Kodabromide F No. 2, Beers 1 with condenser (Omega) 1.50 (32); Beers 1 with diffusion enlarger 1.73 (53). Coated lens used in both tests.

SIGNIFICANCE OF TESTS: Depending on the choice of developers, we may obtain with this No. 2 paper an effective range of anywhere from 1 to 22 to 1 to 58. The normal exposure scale (with Beers 4) of 1 to 32 can be approximated with both No. 1 and No. 3 papers by the use of Beers 7 and Beers 1 respectively. Also, the difference between effective exposure scales with condenser and diffused-light enlargers on the same paper and Beers 1 is considerable—1 to 32 and 1 to 53 respectively. But it is important to note here that the inherent contrast from a condenser enlarger can be canceled out by internal reflections from the bellows, and by flare from an uncoated lens or a dirty lens.

These figures represent only one test. Do not expect to get the same figures with any test you might make yourself. You make it to determine the properties of the paper under your working conditions and expressive requirements.

7. The Weston Step Wedge. This enlarged image shows perceptible tone in step 19 and maximum tone in step 4. Subtracting the wedge densities (not the reflection densities of the print), we get the effective exposure scale of the paper. In this case the respective densities were 1.74 and 0.32; the effective exposure range is 1.42 (about 26 in arithmetic units). Both paper grade and the developer used determine the effective exposure scale.

It is my opinion that the photographer need not devote much time to the theoretical study of paper curves. The exposure range can be determined in terms of practical necessity—with varying amounts of restrainer, and with different developers—by the simple tests described below. Reference to standard technical works will show paper curves and provide explanation of the theory of tone reproduction. However, as I have said, production of expressive prints depends to the full extent upon visual appraisal of their tonal values. Exposure and development of the negative justify far greater mechanical control than need be expended on the print. As pointed out on page 19, the exposure range of the paper and the brilliancy range of the completed print are not directly related; papers of 1 to 10 and 1 to 100 total exposure range may both produce a brilliancy range of 1 to 50. A negative, on the other hand, may be exposed to a subject of tremendous brightness range and by proper development have its opacity range brought within a relatively close span of values (a scale of values directly related to the exposure scale of the paper to be used). Conversely, a subject of very low brightness range may be "expanded" in the negative by exposure and development control. The important difference lies in the fact that while the negative can be given any degree of development required to gain the desired opacity range, the print *must* have full, or near-full, development to preserve good visual qualities in the deeper tones.

As a practical criterion I base my concept of adequate development of the print on the solidity of the blacks in the image. When this degree of development is achieved, and the light values of the image are satisfactory, I feel that the practical optimum of development for that particular print is approached.

If I continue development beyond this optimum, I find the following effects:

1. With chloride papers (Azo, Apex, Convira, etc.), optimum development is rather rapidly achieved, and further development results in the curves moving in entirety to the left (see Fig. 8). In practical terms, this means that while the blacks change little after optimum development, the whites are progressively lowered in tone. A somewhat similar effect would be gained if more exposure had been given the print or if the print emulsion speed had been increased.

2. With bromide papers (Brovira, Royal Bromide, etc.), the change in the curves due to more-than-optimum development is somewhat like changes in the curves of negative materials; the curves increase in slope while moving but slightly to the left (see Fig. 9).

3. With chlorobromide papers (Velour Black, Kodabromide, Cykora, etc.), the changes in the curves due to more-than-optimum development are somewhat between those of 1 and 2.

Therefore we may safely state that the practical difference in development effect between chloride and bromide papers is:

1. The chloride papers develop rapidly to maximum density (expressed in the blacks of the image), and with more-than-optimum development, the lighter values tend to deepen in tone. Effectively, with prolonged development the brilliancy range of the image is reduced: the print appears "softer" and has a depressed quality in the high values.

14

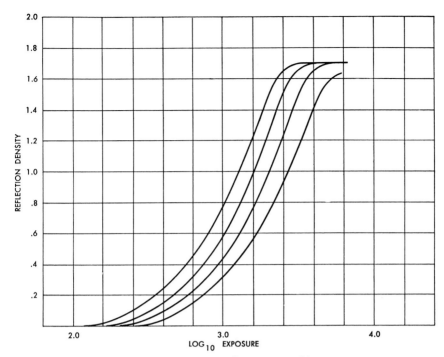

8. Developing Curves for a Chloride Paper. See text, page 14.

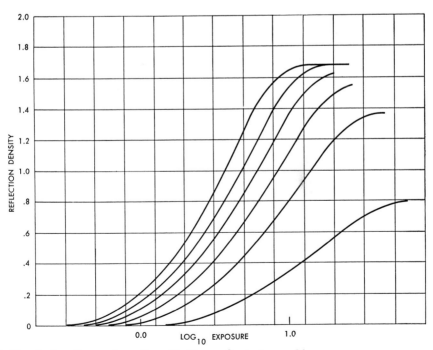

9. Developing Curves for a Bromide Paper. See text, page 14.

2. The bromide papers develop more slowly—both dark and light values increase in density as development approaches the optimum (similar to the development of a negative). Beyond optimum development fog may be produced, and this together with a slight depression of the high values will result in a "graying" of the entire image. It is generally believed that bromide papers should be developed in a somewhat diluted developer; this undoubtedly permits better control and reduces the possibility of fog. But too great dilution may result in inadequate blacks.

3. The chlorobromide papers react between 1 and 2 above, but varieties of this type of paper are not necessarily consistent in their reactions to more-than-optimum development.

Of course in all cases, after the fog point is reached there is a marked depression of the lighter values—but this is due to a different action than the depression of the high values due to more-than-optimum development. In making tests to determine this effect, always have on the exposed strip of paper a small area that has been fully shielded from the printing light; fog will be appraised from this area more definitely than from the areas of lightest tone in the image. Accordingly, be careful not really to *overdevelop!* I think of true overdevelopment as that degree of development in which the first trace of fog is introduced;

10. Farm, Mount Diablo Range, California. In subjects of this type, the relatively small areas of white and black should be rendered intensely against the general average of tone. Note that the buildings are more brilliant than the clouds; the shadowed side of the barn is maximum black. Beers No. 7 was used, and selenium toning further strengthened the blacks.

all other degrees of development—if they achieve the desired results—can be considered correct if not optimum. The manufacturers' instructions for their papers with recommended developers are based on a number of conditions—effective brilliancy scale of the print, print color, efficient developing time, stability, etc. These instructions should not be dismissed, but the creative photographer will soon realize that it will often be advantageous to depart from the norm.

The longer the development, the colder the tone of the print. Some developers —such as the slow-acting Ansco 130 (Metol-glycin-hydroquinone page 112— may require many minutes for optimum development. Dilute Amidol also demands long development times.

The effect of different developing times is suggested in the following test:

TEST FOR EFFECTIVE EXPOSURE SCALES WITH DIFFERENT DEVELOPING TIMES

Data: Kodabromide No. 1, Beers No. 3, (15 cc benzotriazole, (1%) per liter of working developer). Kodak calibrated step wedge (page 18). Exposure constant throughout. Developer temp. 68° F, constant agitation.

	Developing Times	Steps Included in Print	Exposure Range (log.)	Exposure Range (arith.)
Gray, poor blacks, underdeveloped	30 sec.	1 to 14	2.00	100
Still weak blacks, underdeveloped	60 sec.	1 to 15	2.16	145
Still weak blacks, underdeveloped	75 sec.	2 to 17	2.29	195
Good blacks, adequate development	90 sec.	4 to 17	1.99	98
Good blacks, adequate development	105 sec.	4 to 17+	1.99+	98+
More development than necessary for full contrast, the exposure scale reduced	120 sec.	5 to 17	1.83	68
Same as last	150 sec.	6 to 17	1.69	49
Development fog shows, visual contrast low	240 sec.	7 to 18	1.68	48

Significance: The above test is based on simple visual appraisal under normal viewing light. It is only approximate, and does not define the properties of the particular paper used. It shows that the *effective* exposure scale of the paper varies widely depending on amount of development. The objective of a true maximum black is not reached until No. 4 developing time is given. This may be considered the practical effective exposure range of the paper. Additional developing times cannot appreciably deepen the *visual* black of the image but, as will be noted, as more development is given more and more of the less dense steps are submerged in the "ceiling" of tone, while the denser steps, being limited in resolution by the constant exposure, retain their constant value; hence a loss of effective exposure scale.

The last example shows a higher step than the others, because of fog; yet this is illusionary; the effective exposure range is actually less. Just as in Nos. 1, 2, and 3, there is an apparently greater exposure range, but an inadequate visual brilliancy range. It is very important to separate the exposure range of the paper and the brilliancy range of the print image.

A soft paper and a relatively soft developer (with less than normal amount of restrainer) were used to exaggerate the effects.

The effect of different amounts of restrainer added to the developer is suggested in the following test:

TEST FOR EFFECTIVE EXPOSURE SCALES WITH VARYING AMOUNT OF RESTRAINER

Data: Kodabromide No. 1; Beers No. 4; benzotriazole added as per table below. Exposure constant throughout. Kodak calibrated step wedge was used. Developing time adjusted to secure maximum blacks. Developer temp. 68°, constant agitation.

Amount of Benzotriazole (1%) per liter Added to Working Solution	Steps Included in Print	Exposure Range (log.)	Exposure Range (arith.)
25 cc	5-17	1.83	67.5
50 cc	5-16	1.82	66
100 cc	4-15	1.69	49
150 cc	4-14	1.53	34

NOTE: In the above tests I have specified a 1% solution of benzotriazole. Kodak specifies a .4% solution for their antifoggant product. Whatever concentration is used, be certain you apply it consistently to both tests and to the production of prints.

Significance: As restrainer is added to the developer the effective exposure scale is shortened. From 25 to 50 cc per liter, as above, there is not much change. Beyond that amount, the change is quite apparent; the effective exposure scale is halved at 150 cc per liter. This effect could be somewhat neutralized by giving more exposure. (The paper curve is moved to the right as the restrainer content increases.) And for any given exposure value, the addition of restrainer increases contrast.

As potassium bromide is added, the print tone tends toward green. With benzotriazole, etc., the print tone tends toward a bluish value.

This test is only suggestive; it does not define the properties of the paper, and other papers and different developers will give different effects, but the general effect will be somewhat the same in all cases.

NOTE ON STEP WEDGES: These can be made by photographers who are versed in practical sensitometry, but calibrated wedges (tablets) can be purchased, and while their steps may not directly relate to the geometric progressions of the exposure scales (zones), they will, if properly used, accurately demonstrate the exposure scales of papers. The Weston type (Fig. 7, page 13) is circular and adapted to both contact printing and enlarging; the Kodak tablets are continuous and fairly large and are best suited for contact printing.

Brilliancy (Reflection Density)

We must remember that the image in a negative is viewed by transmitted light, and a wide range of opacities may be visually appreciated. The photographic print, however, is viewed by reflected light, and its range of densities (known as reflection densities, or more simply as brilliancies) is determined by the difference between the reflection density of the paper base and that of the surface of the heaviest deposit of silver. Under normal print-viewing conditions a range of 1 to 60 units of brilliancy can but seldom be approached, and for practical considerations the maximum brilliancy range of a glossy print may be considered to be 1 to 50 (reflection density of 1.70). The brilliancy range of a print is not necessarily related to the exposure range of the paper; one paper with an exposure scale of 1 to 10 and another with a scale of 1 to 100 may both, when fully developed, produce prints of the same brilliancy range. In either case a maximum deposit of silver is achieved.

Limitations of Brilliancy of the Print Image

If we could strip a print emulsion from its paper base and examine the image by transmitted light, we would perceive a much greater range of values than in the print itself; transmission densities (opacities) are, generally speaking, greater than reflection densities (brilliancies). Transparencies and lantern slides usually appear of considerably greater scale than the most brilliant print.

It is easy to understand why a print appears so much less "brilliant" than a transparency when we think about the structure of a print image. It consists of a silver deposit on the white-paper base. The silver deposit itself reflects only a small amount of light. We view the image chiefly by the light that passes through it to the paper base, is reflected by the white paper, and again passes through the image to our eyes. Suppose that a given part of the image transmits 1/10 of the incident light (density 1.0, opacity 10). If the white-paper base is capable of reflecting 90% of the light falling on it, the base of the print may then reflect 90% of 1/10 of the light falling on the print surface. But by the time that reflected light on its way back to our eyes has again passed through the silver deposit in that particular portion of the image, it is reduced to only 1/10 of 9%, or 0.9% of the light originally falling upon the print! This reflected light, plus the light reflected from the silver deposit itself, is what the spectator observes as this particular print value. A portion of a print that appears black under moderate illumination may seem only dark gray under stronger light. The intensity of the viewing light may make a profound difference in the appearance—and hence in the emotional effect—of a print. In the section below we see how viewing light must be taken into consideration in the planning of a print.

Viewing Light Intensity

The intensity and color of the light under which prints are seen can reveal or obscure their delicate values. If the viewing light is weak, too little of it is reflected from the dark areas of the print. Subtle values apparent under normal lighting will merely appear black if the intensity of the light reflected from an important dark area of the print falls below the visual threshold. Conversely, this same area may appear insubstantial and characterless if the viewing light is

11. Head of a Nisei Girl, Manzanar, California. (From *Born Free and Equal; the Story of Manzanar*, by Ansel Adams, *U.S. Camera.*) A full-scale print; maximum whites in dress and in highlights on nose, forehead, and lips. General skin textures planned for Zones V-VI, but in making the print they were raised to Zones VI-VII. The print was made on No. 2 Kodabromide, developed in Beers Nos. 5 and 7 (partially developed in No. 5; then completed in No. 7). The print exposure was determined for the desired values of the whites and lighter skin tones; the stronger developer increased the depth of the lower values and the blacks.

20

too strong. Some standard of illumination must be established. I personally prefer to judge my prints with a light equivalent to that of north skylight (between the hours of 10 A.M. and 4 P.M. in summer) with a white-card intensity reading of about 40 on the Weston meter. If the general environmental lighting is very low, the illumination on the print may be substantially reduced to compensate for eye-conditioning to the low environmental illumination. If prints are displayed under tungsten light they will appear warmer in tone than under daylight illumination; the best gallery illumination, to my way of thinking, is a mixture of daylight and tungsten sources. Straight daylight illumination is perhaps too cold for general interior-display effect. (See Book 1, pp. 93-96, for description of the P.S.A. print-viewing box.)

Relating Negatives to Papers

The ideal procedure is to expose and develop negatives so that they will have an opacity scale reasonably related to the exposure scale of the paper to be used. I favor scaling my negatives to a "normal" paper, such as Kodabromide No. 2, or Convira No. 1. However, it frequently happens that a negative will require a paper of longer or shorter scale. (Tests to determine the effective exposure scale of a paper are given on page 12.) If the range of opacity in a negative is 1 to 50, a print is easily obtained on a paper of similar exposure scale. If pure whites are required—as when light sources or bright reflections appear in the image—the opacity range of the negative will be greater. Or if the pure whites are encompassed in the range of 1 to 50, a paper of shorter scale must be used. The pure whites can be represented in the negative as opacities either slightly or greatly above the general range of values (which yield print values from black to the lightest visible gray). A paper of longer exposure scale may reveal some of these higher opacities as light grays in the print.

As we saw in Book 2, the threshold of the negative relates to the faintest perceptible density (opacity) above film-base - plus - fog density; this threshold will appear as almost maximum black in the print in comparison to the uncovered edge of the paper. The threshold of the print emulsion relates to the faintest perceptible value of tone below the white of the paper base. Hence it is logical that we should *print for the whites*—just as we exposed for the shadows when making the negative (see Book 2, pp. 31-35). In the negative, we achieve proper opacities for the higher brightnesses of the subject through development appropriate to the placement on the exposure scale. In the print we achieve desired values for the deep tones and the blacks by selecting the appropriate contrast grade of paper, printing for the whites and, if necessary, altering the composition of the developer or slightly changing the development times. (Ideally, of course, we attempt to design our negative for the type and the grade of paper we intend to use, but some slight control is usually required in the process of printing.)

To sum up: For the negative—expose for the shadows, develop for the high values. For the print—expose for the whites, develop for the blacks.*

When enlargements are made with condenser illumination, the Callier effect apparently increases the contrast in the negative; that is one reason why negatives designed for enlarging with condenser illumination require less development

---

* "Develop for the blacks" should be construed to mean "Adjust the developer formula" rather than to give the print any considerable underdevelopment or overdevelopment in normal developer solutions.

than do negatives designed for contact printing or for enlarging with diffused light. The Callier effect (named for its discoverer) can be explained thus: Whereas *diffuse* light scatters through the negative emulsion in all directions (so that the light which emerges from the negative and passes through the enlarging lens bears a direct relationship to the diffuse densities—or opacities—in the negative image), *collimated* light, being directional, is scattered less by the low opacities of the negative emulsion than by the high opacities. A greater proportion of collimated light is lost by scattering (as distinct from absorption) in the dense portions of the negative. Hence condenser-modified light emerging from the negative emulsion has about the same relative intensity in the shadow values as diffused light, but much less intensity in the high values (high opacities in the negative). There is a formula expressing this difference, but it is hard to apply in practical work. In practical terms, a negative that is to be enlarged with collimated light should be of lower general opacity and of less opacity *range* than a negative designed for contact printing or enlargement with diffused light. (See Book 2, pp. 42 and 90.)

Adjusting the intensity of the contact-printing or enlarging light so that exposures do not exceed 30 seconds, and using a diffuse light source, assures what I consider to be optimum print contrast with a "normal" negative on "normal" paper. Using clear focusing condensers (collimating the light) produces the highest effective contrast. Obviously, between these extremes many degrees of contrast should be possible. Contact printing from a single frosted lamp approaches the same contrast effect as enlarging with a completely diffuse light source. In Book 2 we see that negatives must be designed for the printing process involved; for contact printing a negative requires a higher opacity range than for enlarging with a condenser illuminating system.*

The Weston Analyzer

Although I have often expressed my unfavorable general opinion in regard to the use of photometers in creative printing, I have also qualified my statements, and I do endorse the use of such devices to further the technical command of the medium. I emphasize here their importance in clarifying the problems of paper speeds and effective image brightnesses, in evaluation of the contrast effects of various types of enlargers, and similar problems. I know of no instrument better suited for this purpose than the Weston Fotoval. While it cannot be used as an incident light exposure meter, or as a densitometer (both functions were possible with the obsolete Weston Analyzer) it is far more sensitive than the earlier instrument, and its calibration is intended entirely for its primary use, as a baseboard photometer for print making. The instruction booklet that accompanies the Weston Fotoval is an excellent and thorough treatment of the functions of the instrument; it would serve no purpose to repeat these instructions here. Prospective users of the Fotoval should read the instructions thoroughly, and make all the tests and calibrations called for.

---

* Many of the popular enlargers use condensers in conjunction with frosted lamps, giving a contrast intermediate between fully diffuse and fully collimated light sources. Not only is the contrast affected by the quality of the light source, but the definition of the image suffers if enlargements of high magnification are made with diffused light (unless enlarging lenses of long focal length are used). Conversely, collimated light exaggerates negative grain and image defects.

Choice of Paper Grade When Working with Negatives of Undetermined Opacity Range

While our objective is to "design" a negative for a normal paper grade, we may frequently encounter negatives of different opacity range. With a Weston Fotoval we can easily determine the proper grade of paper to use. Without access to a photometric device, we may select the paper by experience, or by simple trial. We must remember that the usual designation of paper grades are somewhat as follows:

Grade	Number	Exposure Range (log.)	(approx.) (arith.)
Extra-soft	0	2.1	128
Soft	1	1.95	90
Medium soft	2	1.8	65
Medium	3	1.5	30
Medium hard	4	1.3	20
Extra-hard	5	1.2	15

These values imply the full exposure scale of the paper—not merely the "useful scale," as so many manufacturers indicate for their products. (Most published paper-exposure scales are shorter than that listed above, for this reason.) The same grades seldom have the same exposure range in products of different manufacture.

In simple terms, a "soft" negative (one with low opacity range) requires a "hard" paper (one with short exposure range), and vice versa. Just what is the proper grade of paper for an unfamiliar negative may be determined by first printing for the lightest tones (as described on page 62) and then observing the quality of the deepest tones. If the latter are too weak, use a harder grade; if they are too strong, use a softer grade.

Facility in printing from a variety of negatives will come from extensive work; professional photofinishers have an astonishing ability to select the right paper grade for the negative at hand. This empirical approach, however, is not favorable to precisely controlled and expressive work.

Reading a Negative

On the assumption that a print is not merely a "positive of a negative," but an expression or interpretation of the subject photographed, it is important that we know what to print for when working with a negative made by somebody else. In a literal sense, the interpretation of substance and lighting is of supreme importance. My approach to interpretation of a negative is somewhat as follows:

1. I first observe the shadow edges; if they are fairly sharp, I know the lighting is similar to sunlight or ordinary artificial lighting. If they are very sharp, I suspect spotlight illumination. If definite but diffuse, I suspect diffused artificial lighting—such as a lamp in a large reflector placed near the subject. If there is slight or very vague shadow, I know the lighting may be from the open sky, or from highly diffuse lighting in a room, or from large and diffuse reflections.

2. Once I know the kind of lighting employed I am in position to guess what the highlights (specular and semispecular) will tell about the surfaces or substances. If the shadows are fairly sharp (sunlight) and the highlights small and intense, I know the surface is probably smooth and polished. If the sharp highlight is surrounded by a diffuse halo of light, I know the surface is somewhat like varnished wood, brushed aluminum, or the like. If the highlight is dull and diffuse, I know the surface is fairly flat and matte in general quality. It is obvious what the highlight appearances would be with different types of lighting. If a surface shows the reflected image of the lighting source, of course we know it must be mirrorlike. We are further assisted in determining what the substances and surfaces are by connotations of form and texture. A little practice in reading negatives improves our results. Recognizing what the negative reveals of substance and surface in the subject enables us to make more expressive prints.

Print Color

The tones in a so-called black-and-white print are seldom neutral black. In the course of processing, the silver deposit usually assumes a subtle but definite color. Often this color is produced intentionally; many of the commercial papers are designed to yield a yellowish-green black or an olive-green-black tone, both of which are naïvely termed "warm," and are very popular among the portraitists and other professional photographers (not to mention the pictorialists). The following paragraphs on print color will probably provoke considerable discussion. But if they encourage photographers to think more clearly about print color I shall be pleased.

The color of a print image has a profound effect on the apparent depth of tone. It is a well-known psychological fact that certain colors are definitely *aggressive* in character—that is, they appear to advance toward the spectator and float in front of the plane of the image of which they are a part. Other colors are exactly the opposite; I think of them as *recessive*.

Whether or not our awareness of aggressive or recessive colors stems from ancestral experience of selection or whether there is some actual physio-optical effect on the retina, the fact remains that certain colors seem to advance through the plane of the image toward us, while other colors rest behind it. For example, if we study a print of warm-yellow sepia tone (as given by the sulfide toning process) we are impressed by the submergence of the image in this aggressive color. If the color becomes colder—more toward purple—it recedes and seems to exist *behind* the image, strengthening it and appearing to increase the brilliancy scale. The term "recessive" need not mean passive; for our purposes we may say that a recessive color enhances, but neither dominates nor veils, the image in the print.

Once having recognized the psychological importance of the impact of color, we must then realize the endless possibilities of adjusting print color to mood and interpretation. In my own experience, a very slight application of cold-purple sepia to the ordinary print enhances the richness of the image and the illusion of light. Since the print color of ordinary papers varies from bluish-black to olive-black or brown-black, we rarely achieve a satisfying neutral color without some special treatment—either by adjustment of the developer formula or by subsequent toning or by both.

In papers in which the emulsion lies directly on the paper surface and not on a baryta (clay) coating (as in the great majority of present-day papers), the color, the translucence, and the reflective qualities of the paper itself are of great importance. The emulsion actually sinks into the paper fibers, and achieves an actual physical depth that some workers, notably Paul Strand, consider an essential quality in their prints. Such papers, however, may require waxing or varnishing for a satisfactory revelation of the inherent brilliance of the print.

Each of the many possible special effects may have some potential value, but their application should be carefully considered. In any photographic practice our first concern should be to attain some tangible normal standard; in photographic printing I believe the norm is a clean, neutral-tone, black-and-white print. The photographer should fully explore its possibilities before departing from this norm. Poor toning is worse than none.

The subject of toning is discussed on page 78, and formulas for toning are given on page 116.

Recapitulation

The *exposure* scale of a paper relates to the amount of exposure necessary to produce a full range of tones from the faintest perceived tone below white to the maximum black. The *brilliancy* scale of the print relates to the entire range of its reflectivities (reflection densities), from the pure white of the paper base to the maximum black of the silver deposit. The brilliancy scale actually achieved in a print is definitely modified by variations in exposure and development and by toning, and is apparently modified by mounting, by the intensity of the viewing illumination, and by the general level of environmental illumination and reflection where the print is seen.

The photographer must always guard against a casual approach to his work. Visualization of the final print at the time of exposing the negative is essential; the tendency may be to "trust to luck," but the results of a careless approach will never have the strength and the conviction of a fully controlled procedure.

The Importance of Keeping Records

While it is impossible to depend upon consistent speeds of the same grade and make of paper purchased or used at different times—due chiefly to deterioration by age or humidity, or to differences in manufacture—it is of great value to list on the negative envelope the required exposure, and to indicate the plan of dodging, burning, and developing. This will give at least a set of proportionate values; even with different brands and grades of paper it will serve as a helpful guide. The important listings are:

1. Method of printing or enlarging:
   a. distance and power of printing light, or
   b. enlarger, type of light used, enlarging lens and stop, and degree of enlargement
2. Paper make, surface, and contrast grade
3. Developer, developing times and temperature.
4. Basic exposure. (Dodging takes place during this basic exposure—burning is in addition to it.) See page 66.

12. Nevada Fall, Yosemite Valley. When a picture is largely composed of near-solid blacks and brilliant whites, we cannot expect the ordinary engraving to convey the values with adequate subtlety of tone. In fact, throughout this book qualities of tone and print color are discussed that can rarely be depicted in the reproductions. Hence the reader is urged to think of these reproductions as merely suggesting the values of the original prints—and he should attempt to visualize what the subtle passages of tone should be throughout. This print represents the maximum scale of the paper; the blacks are further accented by selenium toning.

THE DARKROOM

Book 1 of this series presents some basic plans for a noncommercial darkroom of moderate size. These plans are offered only as a suggestion; it is my conviction that the design of a darkroom (or any part of the photographic laboratory) should be suited to the individual person, and to his particular work. I have never seen any other basic laboratory design that is as satisfactory as mine —for me. But I know full well that I could not design an entirely satisfactory laboratory for any other photographer. However, certain fundamentals of laboratory design have general application. The most important requirement is to arrange the dry phases of the process on one side of the darkroom and the wet phases on the other side. If the darkroom must be designed in an L-shape, it is important to make a definite break between the worktable and the sink. The chances for splash damage from the various solutions must never be overlooked.

There is no need to repeat here the description of darkroom and finishing room, nor the rather complete listing of the necessary equipment and chemicals for general photographic work (including the printing and enlarging, mounting, and presentation of prints) as set forth in Book 1. But equipment for contact printing and enlarging is described in considerable detail in this book.

Darkroom Lighting

The darkroom should be provided with safelights that give the maximum amount of illumination without danger of fogging the sensitive materials. Safelights for negative materials are discussed in Book 1. My personal preferences for safelights to be used for print processing are:

1. Over the developing tray for either bromide or chloride papers I use a Wratten OA (yellow-green) safelight, fitted with a 60-watt or 100-watt lamp between 2 and 3 feet above the tray. (This amount of light is in excess of that recommended by the manufacturers, but the proper use of the light is described below. A powerful light may produce excessive heat in the fixture.)

2. Over the worktable and the fixing and washing areas of the sink I use bright ruby lamps, or Wratten No. 1 (orange) safelights with 60-watt to 100-watt lamps, depending on the distance of the light above the table or sink. This gives sufficient illumination for everything but close inspection of the negative, for which a viewing box (see Book 1) is advised. However, if Varigam paper is used, both safelight and general working illumination *must* conform to the manufacturer's specifications (Defender Safelight S-55X; 10-watt lamp at 2 feet or 25-watt lamp at 3 feet).

In printing and enlarging, one of the most important considerations is the intensity of general darkroom illumination. If it is too high or too low, properly judging the values in the print image will be very difficult. All prints "dry down" —that is, appear darker when dry than when in the solutions. If the darkroom illumination and the print-viewing light are too bright, the tendency will be to print too dark, for the wet print, far more brilliant than it will be when dry, looks best under a strong light. On the other hand, if the general illumination and the print-viewing light are too weak, the deeper tones in the print will appear deceptively dark, and the dried print may appear weak and flat. I personally desire as high a level of general and safelight illumination as possible without damaging the sensitive emulsions, and the light by which I inspect fixed prints is a shielded daylight lamp.

The intensity of the OA safelight I use over the developing tray is too high for continuous use. To avoid fogging the print I follow either of these procedures:

1. I have a foot switch to control the safelight, and flash the light on only near the end of development. (The print is less sensitive at this stage than when first immersed in the developer.) The general orange or red darkroom illumination is adequate to observe the progress of development of the print up to the critical point.

2. Or if the safelight is on constantly, up to the critical point I keep the developing tray shielded with a card or a sheet of hard rubber or opaque plastic. I simply remove the card to allow the full safelight illumination to fall on the nearly completed image. Two refinements of this method are:

    a. Use a sheet of transparent orange or red plastic that permits observation of the print throughout development but can be removed for careful inspection of print values during the final stages.

    b. Have the cover hinged to the tray, or to a device in which the tray can rest (a secondary, larger tray to serve as a water jacket and maintain consistent temperature is a most helpful accessory).

A print cannot be judged accurately until it has been fixed; while it is still in the developer the unexposed and undeveloped silver halides in the emulsion have a veiling effect. With experience the photographer can learn to reconcile the difference between the appearance of the print in the developer and its appearance after clearing in the fixing bath and in the wash water. (Some papers show more obvious clearing than others.) The aspect of the print in the developer must be interpreted in terms of its appearance after clearing, when dry, and perhaps also when mounted.* It must always be remembered that any print, regardless of surface, has a much greater brilliance when wet than when dry. Prints of either dull matte on glossy surface may appear practically the same in the fixing bath and the washing tray, but when dry the matte print will show a brilliancy range of about 1 to 15, and the glossy print a range of about 1 to 50. As is shown elsewhere, the only sure method of determining values during the printing process is to work first for the whites of the image and then to adjust exposure and development to achieve the desired blacks.

It is advisable to judge the print after clearing in the fixing bath by the daylight lamp mentioned above. The light must not be too bright, and the print must be held under it in such a way as to avoid reflections. I find that if I first look at the print in full, direct light, then turn it at a very sharp angle to the light— very quickly, so that the eyes do not have time to adapt themselves—the effective brilliance is reduced and I have a better idea of how the print will look when dry.

A satisfactory way to test darkroom illumination is to lay a small strip of the fastest paper to be used face up on the worktable, expose parts of it for various intervals of time, and then develop it fully. For example, if it is progressively uncovered about an inch at a time, at 1-minute intervals, a 5-inch strip

---

* Mounting a print on a white board will subjectively alter its values.

will have areas exposed from 1 to 5 minutes. If on full development this strip shows any fog, it is easy to note what amount of exposure produced it. Even if a 5-minute exposure to the general illumination of the darkroom produces fog, the intensity of this illumination should be reduced. Too much exposure to the safe-light during development of the print may degrade the high values of the image (even if the same safelight exposure to an unprinted sheet would show no fog!). This is because the slight exposure the whites of the print represent is *reinforced* by subsequent exposure to the safelight, and increased density may result.

The same test should be carried out in the development tray under the general illumination of the room. Then a test should be made to see how much of the developing safelight the paper can stand (when the light is controlled as described above). Fog produced by too much illumination should not be confused with fog produced by prolonged development (tests for which are described on page 12).

Inspection should be made to detect any light leaks around the enlarger or through cracks in the safelight boxes. Inspect for these leaks from the position of the paper; a serious leak may not be seen from the normal eye position. A mirror can be used here to good advantage. It must be remembered that safe-lights may in time deteriorate from the heat of the lamps, dampness, etc. I advise frequent testing to preclude the fogging of films and fast papers.

The strong print-viewing light over the fixing tray should never be turned on until the print has entirely cleared—that is, until the slight milkiness in the image has entirely disappeared. Make this visual test: Expose a sheet of paper and develop it fully to get a deep allover gray value; then, at the moment of immersion in the fixing bath, flash on the print-viewing light. The process of clearing can be observed, and it will be seen that the print clears in streaks and blotches. If the fixing bath is slow in action and the light very bright, these streaks may show as permanent markings (the previously unexposed silver halides are affected by the bright light, and the small amount of developer remaining in the emulsion develops them enough to produce streaks on the print).

Darkroom Precautions

Unwanted chemical action on prints should be guarded against by cleanliness, careful storage of papers—either unexposed or finished—in cool and dry places, and the avoidance of rust. A chipped porcelain-coated iron tray, for instance, should be painted over (or better, discarded). Developers that stand in trays exposed to air for any length of time oxidize, and stains result when prints come in contact with the products of oxidation.

Prolonged immersion of prints in stop baths or fixing solutions may weaken the lighter values in the images, and unfortunate effects frequently result from excessive heat in drying. To protect the print from possible blistering and frilling, there should be no great or sudden variations in the temperature of the solutions during processing.

In making up solutions for processing, mix all ingredients in the order in which they are listed in the formula, and be certain that each substance is thoroughly dissolved before the next is added. In most formulas, the use of chemicals of good quality dissolved in pure water, together with accurate preparation, should result in a clear solution with little or no sediment. Should the mixture remain clouded, or should suspended crystals appear, it must be assumed that

13. The Grand Canyon, Arizona. In complex subjects such as this, either the whites or the blacks should be exaggerated, to accentuate the natural patterns. In this case the blacks are intentionally printed well below their normal value. In the negative (and in a strictly representational print from it) the shadows are placed at about Zones II-III, but in this print they appear on Zone I and below. However, in the fine print there is a trace of texture showing in the shadows—more than would obtain were the shadows exposed on Zone I on the negative. Were this picture made into a large mural, the shadow values would not be printed as deep as they appear here; the increased size of the shadowed areas would demand a certain amount of texture. Were the shadows exposed on Zone I or below (on the negative), it would be necessary to print them to Zone I or lower in the print, as there is nothing more unpleasant than a textureless area printed to insufficient depth of tone.

something has gone amiss. A few formulas, such as parts of the Nelson gold-toning solutions show definite cloudiness, but the instructions tell how to use them. Many concentrated stock solutions crystallize at low temperatures, but this effect should be no cause for concern unless the crystals persist above 68° F.* No print should be immersed in a developer until all crystallized matter is completely dissolved; otherwise dark spots are almost certain to appear on the print. When ordinary tap water is used for mixing developer solutions, some of the ingredients may form colloidal precipitates with substances present in the water; it is advisable to filter the solutions made with this water. Also, it is a good plan to swab all prints thoroughly before the final rinse and drying. Except when tap water is unusually pure, it is advisable to mix all solutions in distilled water; water with a high chlorine content can be particularly troublesome. Discard baths when any cloudiness or sludge appears.

Needless to say, all containers, graduates, trays, tongs, and fingers should be clean and free of contaminating chemicals. Practically all print developers (Amidol excepted) are strongly alkaline; slopping any of the acid stop bath or fixing solution into the developer seriously affects its alkalinity and depresses its activity. It is important to set up a routine of cleanliness in all darkroom procedures; fingers that have been immersed in stop bath or fixing bath *must* be rinsed in clean water before they touch towels, developer, or prints. Further, they must be *thoroughly* dried before they touch negatives or printing paper; drops of water on the surface of the paper before printing or development may ruin the print, and serious harm may result from transmission of any moisture to the negative. Should a drop of water fall on a negative during the printing process, a spot is sure to result unless the negative is immersed immediately in fresh water and allowed to stand for at least 15 minutes, then rinsed and hung to dry. Should a drop of *developer* fall on the negative, that negative must be put quickly into the stop bath, then into the fixing bath, and then washed thoroughly; otherwise a stain may eventually appear. Should a drop of water or developer lie between negative and paper emulsions while the two are tightly pressed together in the printing frame, physical damage to the negative is practically certain.

Equipment for Contact Printing

The requirements for contact printing are extremely simple. Unless great numbers of prints are to be made (see page 99), the ordinary printing frame used with an overhead light is the most efficient and satisfactory method of contact printing. Figure 14 is a simple diagram of such an ensemble. The printing frame is merely a metal or wooden frame of adequate size holding a sheet of very clear and perfect glass (any bubble or scratch would show in the print), and having a padded back that is secured by spring tongues to assure firm and even contact of the printing paper with the emulsion side of the negative.

It is interesting to note that the hinged back of the conventional printing frame is a relic of the days of printing-out papers; the paper was firmly held against the negative by pressure of either part of the back, and the progress of

---

* It is important to remember that if crystals have formed and settled to the bottom of the bottle, the composition of the remaining liquid is no longer the same; hence it is important to immerse the container in warm water, raise the temperature of the solution, stir, and see that all crystals are redissolved before the liquid is used. (Glacial acetic acid has the common property of expanding as it solidifies and may break the bottle if it falls below 60° F.)

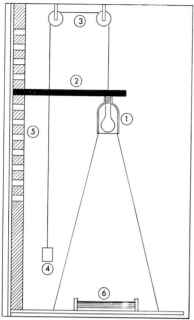

1. Printing light (frosted lamp in ventilated housing with piece of ground or opal glass before the lamp.) Light must be perfectly even over entire printing area. 2. Square (1x1) rod supporting the lamp—to fit in square openings in 5. This supporting rod may be attached to a sliding bar on 5, which may be clamped at any position. The rod and lamp are counterbalanced by the weight 4, attached by a stout cord that runs over the pulleys 3. 5. A stout piece of wood (about 2x2 and of appropriate height) in which rectangular holes are cut to take the lamp-supporting rod. Or this can be designed to hold a sliding bar (to which is attached the lamp-supporting rod), which can be clamped at any height. On 5 should be attached a clearly visible scale showing the distance, at any position, of the ground or the opal glass of the printing lamp to the plane of the negative in the printing frame. 6. A regular contact-printing frame, equipped with a perfect piece of glass, a thin sponge-rubber sheet to go between back of paper and back of printing frame, and a guide on the table to assure correct position of the frame under the lamp.

14. Schematic Diagram of a Contact-Printing Assembly. Designed for "overhead" printing with a printing frame. This method permits extensive control by dodging and burning, and also provides for great variation of intensity of the printing light (by altering its distance from the printing frame). Description of the various parts of this assembly is given above.

printing could be observed by merely opening the other part and bending out the released portion of the print.

In the modern printing frame this feature is retained, but it should be noted that if the edges of the frame supporting the glass are given a slight *inward* bevel, acute reflections of light to the paper will be avoided.

The reader should be reminded that the inverse-square law holds in regard to the distance of the light from the printing frame; hence a range of 1 to 4 in distance from light to frame results in a range of 1 to 16 in effective printing-light intensity.

The use of a thin sponge-rubber cushion between the paper and the back of the printing frame assures even pressure of paper against negative and negative against glass—thereby minimizing the appearance of Newton's rings (interference patterns due to minute air spaces, moisture, or merely unequal contact between negative and glass). Their patterns may not be noticeable in the print in areas of complex texture, but can be very distressing when they appear in the sky or other continuous-tone areas of the image. They can sometimes be observed as iridescent areas under the glass if the loaded printing frame is held at a favorable angle under the safelight. If they persist in the sky areas, placing the negative in another position in the frame may avoid the conditions giving rise to rings. The rings also show in enlargements when the negative is held between two pieces of glass, especially if the negative has a slight tendency to buckle.

Although conventional printing boxes appear efficient, they have one great disadvantage: dodging or burning (see page 66) of the print during exposure may be carried out only by a rather complicated insertion of light-absorbing tissues between the negative and the printing lights. The most satisfactory printing boxes are the fairly elaborate and expensive commercial types containing 6, 9, 12, or more lights, each controlled by a separate switch, and having above the lights one or more ground-glass trays on which light-absorbing tissues can be placed as required. Ordinary tissue paper in single or multiple folds works very well for decreasing the intensity of light over certain areas of the film, but it must be placed far enough from the negative so that it casts no well-defined shadow edges on the print. The use of such elaborate printing boxes is practical only when quantities of prints are to be made from one negative (see page 99), since preparing the device for the ideal exposure may be a rather lengthy process. However, once the right combination of lights and masking tissues is established, any number of identical prints can be produced.

If fast bromide or chlorobromide papers are to be used, it is quite satisfactory to place an ordinary printing frame under any standard enlarger and direct the enlarger light on it. Figures 15a and 15b show a comparison between a contact print made in this way and an enlargement made through the same enlarger—both on the same paper and from the same negative.

As most papers (excepting Varigam) are sensitive only to blue light, fast bromide and chlorobromide papers can be used for contact printing with amber light; the paper is affected chiefly by the blue residuals passing through the amber globe. This type of light minimizes the effects of slight yellow stains in the negative.

A printing frame is an essential item in any photographer's equipment, as contact prints should be made from each negative as a matter of record, whether the final print is to be contact or enlargement. "Proof" prints on contact printing-out paper reveal the full range of values in the negative (see page 4).

15a. Leaf Pattern. Enlarged about 1:1 on Velour Black No. 2, glossy. Beers No. 5.

15b. Same. Contact-printed by enlarger light on the same paper. Both prints developed together.

For enlarging negatives of ordinary size ($3\frac{1}{4}$x$4\frac{1}{4}$ up to 8x10), I believe it is hard to improve on a simple horizontal enlarger using diffused illumination. I do not disparage vertical enlargers, as they certainly have many practical advantages, but a horizontal enlarger can be assembled easily, using a standard view camera (and without impairing the regular use of such camera). A good electrician—understandably one who is versed in modern lighting problems—can make up a mercury-argon grid or a bank of fluorescent tubes, and the lighthousing and camera support as well as the overhead easel can be produced by a capable cabinetmaker. The cost should be much less than that of a first-rate vertical enlarger. Fluorescent tubes (sufficiently close in a curved bank), a grid of mercury-argon tubing, an M Cooper-Hewitt mercury-vapor tube (or 2 U tubes side by side), or a simple bank of frosted tungsten lamps—any of these is satisfactory if properly diffused and adequately ventilated.

A simple horizontal enlarger consists essentially of a lighttight illumination box containing the diffusion glasses and having lightproof ventilation, and a negative carrier with various kits for different negative sizes. The camera is placed in front of the above assembly, and the entire apparatus is supported by a simple but rigid shelf. Such a design is suggested in Fig. 16. While the view camera or any camera of similar type with detachable back can be adapted as the enlarging camera (by having a lightproof flange made in which the camera can rest), it will be well to procure a standard enlarging lens, since the ordinary lens, no matter how good it may be for general work, is seldom adequate for critical enlarging use. A process-type lens is advised.

Camera, negative carrier, and easel should be designed and assembled so that the negative is precisely parallel to the paper on the easel, both *horizontally and vertically*, and the axis of the lens must be perpendicular to both the plane of the negative and the plane of the paper. Focusing and magnification scales for approximate settings (to be perfected by examination of the image on the easel) can easily be attached to both camera and easel. Details of arrangement are more fully discussed in Book 1. I have a personal preference for horizontal enlargers, but I realize that limitations of space may make the vertical enlargers far more practical for many photographers.

Glassless negative carriers are advised for all types of enlargers, as scratches and other defects accumulate on glass as well as on the negative surfaces, whereas in glassless carriers there are only the two surfaces of the negative to contend with. Further, glass carriers often are troublesome because of Newton's rings (page 32). If the negative has a strong tendency to buckle, of course glass must be used; even so, the surface of the negative should not touch the surfaces of the glasses. A thin (1/16 inch) cardboard mask can be inserted on either side of the negative; it will prevent contact of the negative with the glasses and at the same time keep buckling within safe limits. Also, glass must be used in vertical enlargers if the negatives have a tendency to sag.

For controlling the duration of exposure it is convenient to have a shutter mounted in the lens, but it is equally effective to use a lens cap, or if the enlarger is horizontal, simply a small piece of cardboard leaned against the lens. Some workers prefer a foot switch for the enlarger light; others choose an electrical timing device. If fluorescent or gaseous discharge tubes are used, the light should

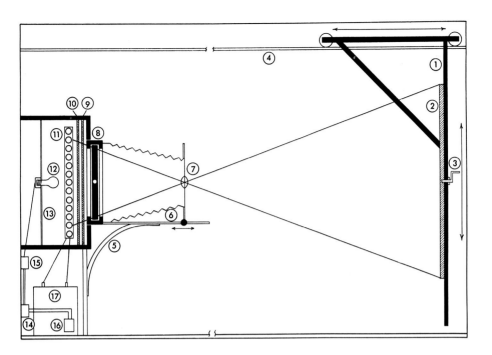

16. Schematic Diagram of a Horizontal Enlarger Assembly. Designed for regular and (with sufficient space in the darkroom) photomural enlarging. This plan assumes that a standard view camera will be used as the enlarging camera, without impairing use of the camera for regular work. The back assembly of the camera must be removed, and the camera body fitted snugly into lightproof grooves of the lamphouse frame. Description of the various parts of this assembly follows: 1. Easel frame, which slides or rolls on overhead tracks (4), and may be clamped in any position. 2. The easel, a slab of soft wood to which the paper can be attached directly by thumbtacks, or which will hold a special printing frame or paper holder. This easel is attached by: 3. A clamp that sets the easel in any desired position; the easel may be raised or lowered through a slot cut in 1, or rotated on the plane of the image. A tilting assembly (to correct or produce distortions) could be made without undue complications. 5. Shelf-bracket support for enlarging camera. 6. Camera. It should rest on a sturdy support, and one not too wide to interfere with the focusing knob. 7. Enlarging lens. Should be centered with the center of the negative, and mounted in strict alignment with the plane of the negative. (Easel plane and negative plane must be in accurate alignment at all positions.) 8. Negative holder and frame. 9. Ground or opal glass. 10. Clear glass. Space between 9 and 10 should be vented with lightproof louvers or tubes. 11. Bank of tubes, or grid. 12. Photoflood lamp (for focusing only). 13. White background of lamphouse (should be slightly curved for maximum evenness of light). 14. Main input for lamp current. 15. Switch for Photoflood lamp. 16. Switch for bank of tubes or grid. 17. Transformer for grid (usually of high voltage; be certain it is safely shielded). The wall surfaces near the enlarger assembly should be painted a dark and nonreflective color to minimize fog from scattered light. With very big enlargements, the image may "spill" over to the wall and reflect light back on the paper. If this occurs, the lens should be shielded.

remain on and the exposure should be controlled by the shutter, cap, or card, because the intensity of the light may vary from the norm for a short time after the current is turned on and consistent intensity of light is not assured if the light is turned on and off repeatedly. Electrical timers have certain advantages when many enlargements are to be made from the same negative; personally I find them unnecessary, and difficult to use if dodging or burning is required. I prefer to use a metronome for timing my prints and enlargements.

For considerable enlargement from very small negatives, it is advisable to use a condenser enlarger, for collimated light favors sharpness of image, especially with short-focus lenses.

The vertical type of enlarger—mostly designed for condenser illumination—has become increasingly popular, and there are many good types. It conserves horizontal space, but the height of the darkroom ceiling must be considered in planning for a vertical enlarger. The ideal type is that in which either diffused or condenser illumination can be obtained by use of interchangeable parts (the Kodak Precision Enlarger, for example). There should be some means of turning the enlarger assembly on its support from the vertical to the horizontal position, so as to permit making enlargements requiring greater lens-to-easel distance than is possible in the vertical position.

The Eastman Auto-focus enlargers and the Saltzmann enlargers are among the highest type of professional equipment. The Omega and the Solar enlargers are excellent in the condenser-illumination field. But beware the poorly constructed enlarger; there are all too many on the market.

For special work, tilting easels have many advantages. See PHOTO-LAB-INDEX, Section 17, p. 30.

Lenses for Enlarging Purposes

Lenses designed for enlarging are always to be preferred; however, for ordinary work any well-corrected anastigmat of adaptable focal length may be acceptable, although it will usually be necessary to use a moderately small aperture for adequate coverage and flatness of field. A process-type lens is undoubtedly superior—and is essential for making enlargements in color photography.

The enlarging lens is capable of producing flare, just as any camera lens is (Books 1 and 2), and it is certain that a coated lens enhances the brilliance of the projected image. In order to see how greatly the enlarged image can be affected by internal flare, place in the negative holder a piece of cardboard from which a circle about 1-inch diameter has been cut out. Make a projection print of the image of this circle, exposing for approximately the time required for an ordinary negative. Not only will the print show a definite flare around the image of the circular cutout, but a general allover fog will probably show also. When we enlarge negatives in which there are large areas of low density, we are certain to find a similar degradation of the lighter values of the image. The same test carried out with a coated lens will yield a superior image, demonstrating the value of optical coating of enlarger lenses. Of course *camera flare* (reflections from the interior of the enlarging camera) must be considered; an adjustable baffle within the camera (back of the lens) will reduce this flare.

In addition to lens flare, dust and finger marks have deleterious effects on the image. In vertical enlargers the upper surface of the lens should be cleaned frequently, as dust settles on it from above.

The amount of "travel" of the lens required for various magnifications can be computed from the simple formulas in Section 17 of the PHOTO-LAB-INDEX, from which we can establish the bellows draw required in the camera and the necessary distance to the enlarging easel. The longer the focal length of the enlarging lens, the better definition and coverage it affords; however, choice of equipment must be determined by available space.

In using a horizontal enlarger, it is better to mount the paper on an easel suspended from the ceiling and to move it in relation to the enlarging camera (when adjusting the size of the image and the approximate focus) rather than to employ a fixed easel and move the camera assembly. Such an easel is simple to construct; mounted on two parallel and accurately horizontal overhead wooden tracks, it can be braced in a perfectly vertical position by diagonal assembly bars with firm wing-nut adjustments. The easel itself should be square, its dimensions exceeding the greatest dimensions of the enlargements to be made (so as to allow for placement of the paper at any position). On this easel there should be a secondary panel of soft wood to which the paper can be fastened with thumbtacks. If this panel is mounted by means of a clamp nut extending through a vertical slot in the easel itself, it can be raised or lowered or rotated. Then slight adjustments in the position of the image will not necessitate raising or lowering the negative carrier, or raising or lowering the lens, for the soft wood panel carrying the paper can be raised, lowered, or turned as required. Hence the axis of the lens need not be moved from the center of the negative. The position of the image can be adjusted horizontally by merely moving the negative carrier in the enlarger assembly. But since this displaces the center of the negative in relation to the lens axis, it will be better to place the enlarging paper at the required position on the panel.

Another advantage of the horizontal-enlarger assembly (in addition to its potentially greater projection space) is that the ceiling-suspended easel can be pushed to the extreme end of the worktable when not in use, leaving more free working space for other purposes. Huge enlargements—such as photomural sections—obviously demand horizontally arranged apparatus and adequate projection space.

While in horizontal enlarging the extreme corners of the paper can be pinned to the easel, there is always the danger of buckling and curling, which produces uneven depth of field, and results in impaired definition in parts of the image. Unless some framing device is used to hold the paper on the panel, a thin metal strip along the bottom of the panel, with about a 1/16-inch gap along its entire length (such gap about ⅛-inch deep) will adequately hold the bottom edge of the paper against the board. A few thumbtacks (preferably the long aluminum pushpins) will secure the top corners (and the edges if needed). Insert the pins so that they lean *out;* otherwise they may throw a shadow on the edge of the image.

The use of glass over the paper will hold it flat, but of course every scratch, bubble, or speck of dust in or on the glass is a potential troublemaker. I prefer to use a simple wooden frame the full opening of which is ½ inch less (in each dimension) than the size of the paper used. This gives me a margin of ¼ inch all around. The frame is hinged at the bottom, and opens far enough so that the paper can easily be set against supporting pins (which conveniently determine the margins). When the frame is closed, these pins nest in holes in the back, and the frame is clamped firmly with a spring finger at the top, which holds the paper securely along the edges. Only in extreme cases is there any forward buckling of the center area of the paper.

17. Boulder Dam (Hoover Dam), California. A normal-soft negative, printed to preserve the illusion of light. While the clouds were actually whiter than the concrete of the dam, they were slightly burned down so that the emotional effect of the brilliancy of the dam would be preserved. Actually, the dam related to about Zone VII and the clouds to Zone VIII. There was no way to control these values directly; careful burning of the sky section of the image during printing was required—and especial care was necessary to avoid darkening of the upper part of the transmission tower. Under most normal outdoor conditions, shadows in the foreground are deeper in tone than distant shadows (under identical quality of illumination), due to atmospheric effects. Hence the shadows on the distant hills would not be as deep as the shadows near the tower. If the upper part of the picture was burned in to favor the clouds, and the shadowed hills then rendered too dark, the effect would be illogical and definitely "phony."

Standard adjustable easels for use with vertical enlargers consist of a base and a metal top assembly holding all edges of the paper firmly to the baseboard. Ideal in principle, these easels seldom give accurately rectangular margins. *Only one* of the many easels of this type I have used has been accurate! I have also found that many of the easels of this type have rounded or beveled edges on one or two sides in contact with the paper; these edges, although painted black, may not be a completely matte black, and have the unfortunate property of reflecting light onto the paper and producing thin black lines in the lighter areas of the image. This effect is produced when marginal parts adjacent to the paper are beveled outward; these bevels should be directed slightly *inward*. Further, all parts should be painted a dead matte black to minimize reflections.

The usual white surface of the easel is excellent to focus upon, but with single-weight enlarging papers enough light may pass through the paper and reflect back from the white surface to produce an appreciable fogging effect on the print. This is evidenced by a faint "halo" effect around intensely black lines and edges in the image. A backing of dark cardboard should always be used with single-weight papers; I do not consider it necessary with double-weight papers.

Some enlargers have swing and tilt adjustments of both lens and negative carrier, enabling the photographer to correct rectilinear distortions in the negative. These are of considerable value for negatives made with cameras that do not possess standard adjustments. A carpenter's simple protractor level is helpful in aligning negative plane and easel plane. This subject is adequately treated elsewhere (PHOTO-LAB INDEX, Section 17), but it must be stressed here that if distortions are corrected in enlarging, the proportions of the subject may be altered. For example, a distorted image of a square form may be corrected to rectilinear accuracy, but the form will then appear as a rectangle, wider than high (or vice versa, depending on the direction of distortion), rather than as a square. Control of perspective effects in enlarging is termed *variography*.

Enlargers should be grounded to minimize collection of dust due to electrostatic charges. Dust should be removed frequently with a good camel's-hair brush, and from the inside of the enlarger with a vacuum cleaner.

Dodging and burning apparatus is described on page 67. See Book 1 for further description of essential equipment and accessories.

Focusing

Focusing the image on the easel deserves careful consideration. If intense illumination is used and if the lens is of process type, the image is focused easily at maximum lens aperture without the use of a focusing magnifier. However, under other conditions the following procedures may be required:

1. With low-intensity illumination, or if the eye does not function well a reading distance, a focusing magnifier (such as the new Bausch and Lomb Enlarging Focusing Magnifier—Catalog No. 81–34–53) is very helpful. This instrument gives considerable magnification; the grain of the image can be sharply focused. It is adjusted for "infinity" focus of the eye; if glasses are used for distance, they must also be used with this magnifier. For special cases a compensating eye-piece could be prepared.

2. Many lenses not designed for "process" or enlarging work are used in enlarging cameras. In these the critical focus may change slightly when the lens is stopped down, therefore be sure to check the focus at the aperture to be used in making the enlargement.

3. If the negative has any tendency to buckle, a relatively small aperture must be used, or the enlarged image will not be consistently sharp.

4. It will be found helpful to insert along the edge of the negative holder, precisely on the plane of the emulsion of the negative, a section of a lined pattern—transparent lines on a black field, or vice versa (such specially designed patterns are available). Critical focus can be established for such a pattern much more easily than for the negative image itself, especially with illumination of low visual intensity.

Even Illumination

It will be remembered that the image is less brilliant toward the edges of the field of any lens than at the center of the field. There is some truth in the conventional statement that the same lens should be used for enlarging the negative as was used for making the negative, as the reduced brilliance of the edges of the negative would be automatically canceled out. However, this does not apply when only part of the negative is being enlarged. I repeat that in enlarging it is generally best to use a lens of as long a focal length as practical; I find it results in a gratifying crispness and precision of image, as well as evenness of illumination.

When enlargements from miniature negatives are so large that grain is apparent, it is quite important that the grain be rendered with equal sharpness over the entire area of the picture. In this case the *illusion of definition* depends largely upon the consistent sharpness of the grain image (see Book 1, p. 35, and Book 2, p. 88).

Evenness of illumination in condenser-type enlargers must not be taken for granted. A condenser system includes a light source, the condensers, and the enlarging lens. The focal length of the lens determines both its distance from the negative and the proper position of the light with respect to the condensers. In order to achieve a perfectly even field of illumination, the entire system must be in correct optical relationship—the proper positions of the light and the condensers will be different for each position of the lens in reference to the plane of the negative. In the standard models of miniature enlargers the condenser systems are corrected for all normal degrees of enlargement with the lens specified for the equipment. In the larger models there is usually a handy method of adjusting the position of the light. When negative, lens, and easel are set to give the required image, the negative can be withdrawn from the enlarger, and the field of illumination on the easel can be appraised for consistent brilliance over the entire image area. The light and the condenser can then be adjusted before the negative is replaced and the enlargement is made.

Evenness of illumination of a diffused-light system is inherent in the design and construction of the system. A bank of fluorescent tubes, or a close grid of mercury-argon tubes, backed with an efficient reflecting surface, is ideal. The tube system must be high enough and wide enough to provide a perfectly even area of illumination when the lens is in the closest possible position to the negative (the

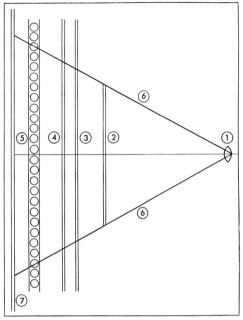

1. The lens; it should be of adequate focal length and quality to cover the negative fully.

2. The negative; between glass, or in a glassless carrier.

3. Sheet of ground or opal glass; it must be at sufficient distance from the negative to avoid any possible granular image showing when the lens is stopped down.

4. Sheet of plain glass. Space between 2 and 3 serves as a ventilation area; it should be vented by lightproof louvers or tubes.

5. Bank of tubes, or grid of continuous tubing (spaced as closely as possible). This space should also be ventilated by lightproof louvers.

6. Angle of illumination necessary to cover negative. (Note oversize light field.)

7. Highly reflective background (preferably slightly concave). A Photoflood lamp (on a separate switch) may be mounted in the center of this background for focusing purposes.

18. Schematic Diagram of Enlarger Illumination (diffused light). The all-important elements of the enlarger system are shown here. It will be noted that the illumination field exceeds the angle of view through the negative. This is intentional, as the light at the edges and the corners of the field will "fall off" in intensity unless there is ample illumination along the borders of the field. Curving of the reflective background (7) will also balance the illumination. Description of the various elements is given above.

position for greatest enlargement). Figure 18 shows schematically the relative positions of light, negative, and lens, and indicates the importance of suitable intensity of illumination over the entire field.

A bank of tungsten lamps can be used if their light is so diffused that no "hot spots" are visible (one or more sheets of opal diffusing glass will be required). A bank of electric lamps is certain to produce considerable heat, and ventilating spaces should be provided between glasses—adding clear glasses, if necessary, to an adequate set of diffusing glasses. If the heat is excessive, a sheet of heat-absorbing glass, such as Corning Aklo glass, is advised.

Many devices have been presented to the photographic world to give an even source of diffused light. In my opinion, nothing excels a grid of mercury-argon tubing (smallest standard tubing, bent together as closely as possible and mounted against a white-enamel board). It will require the use of a high-voltage transformer, but the entire equipment can be made to order by a competent electrician for a relatively low price. The light is highly actinic, but of low visual intensity; hence I recommend that a Photoflood lamp be used for focusing. At one time I used two Cooper-Hewitt M-shaped tubes, one behind the other and slightly offset, with satisfactory results. It gave very even illumination with one sheet of clear glass and one sheet of opal glass between the tubes and the negative; the space between the glasses was cooled by two lightproof ventilating tubes.

The diffusing glass should be far enough from the negative so that no texture of its surface can possibly come into focus, even when the lens is stopped down.

Not only the quality, but also the intensity, of the enlarging light is important, because reciprocity departure affects paper emulsions in much the same way as it affects negatives (see Book 2, p. 13).

Intensity of light. There is a definite relationship between the intensity of the image projected on the sensitive paper emulsion and the effective contrast in an enlargement (or a print). If the projected image is of low intensity, because of 1) low intensity of the light source, 2) small aperture of the enlarging lens, or 3) high opacity of the negative, the contrast in the enlargement may be different from what one would expect that particular negative (and paper) to produce.

The first evidence of reciprocity failure is found in the highlights of the print image. At a certain intensity of the projected image there may be a normal satisfactory balance between dark and high values in the print, with a fine gradation of subtle tones shown in the high values. As the intensity of the image is lessened (because of a greater degree of enlargement, lower intensity of the light source, a smaller aperture of the enlarging lens, or a greater distance from printing light to printing frame), the high values are the first to suffer; they become blocked and chalky, because the intensity of illumination in these areas is insufficient to affect the sensitive silver grains adequately. Hence gradation is lost— that is, the transition from middle to high values is too abrupt—and the quality of the image suffers. If the intensity of the image is further reduced, the reciprocity-failure effect includes lower values in the print; with very low intensity of the projected image, the entire scale of values in the print is affected. It is then difficult to get adequate blacks even if the time of exposure is lengthened sufficiently to print through the whites. The characteristics of the paper emulsion are in effect severely changed, the straight-line section being lengthened and the contrast in the paper being considerably reduced. The Eastman Kodak Company has advised me that a full-scale print should not have more than 60 seconds' exposure if the characteristics of the paper are to be fully retained.

Thus we see that if the intensity of the image which falls on the paper is seriously reduced—because of high negative density, small lens aperture, excessive enlargement, or (in contact printing) great distance from light to printing frame—the intensity of the light source must be increased to compensate.

If, however, we can discover by practical test just how reciprocity failure affects contrast in the print or the enlargement, we have an additional element of control at our disposal. Remember: The first effects of reciprocity departure favor increase in print-image contrast; beyond this, though, the contrast is lessened.

Collimated Light

Not all enlargers collimate light to the same extent. Among possible arrangements are: 1) a point source used with clear condensers, giving the most uniformly directional light and the most contrasty image; 2) a condenser system together with a frosted lamp, giving what I term "normal" condenser effect; 3) a frosted lamp used with a condenser system having one or more of the surfaces frosted (ground), and giving the softest effect possible with condensers. As a practical example of the relative contrast obtained with the above types and a diffused-light source, I once made three enlargements from the same negative, one in each of three types of enlarger. With the first I used No. 1 Kodabromide paper. Next, I placed the negative in a standard Omega, and got a good print with No. 2 Kodabromide. Then I used my mercury-argon diffused-light enlarger, and had to resort to No. 3 Kodabromide. The smoothest effect was with the diffused-light enlarger; the harshest effect and the greatest evidence of grain, scratches, and other defects appeared in the print made with the most highly collimated light.

I am sure that the serious photographer will realize the futility of rules regarding developing times and gamma and will understand the desirability of making his own tests in application to his own equipment and methods—from exposure meter and camera through printing procedures and enlarging, and taking into account his personal concept of print values and expressive qualities. And I am convinced that the photographers who wish to preserve a consistent quality through all their prints will find it worth while to concentrate on one type (and perhaps one brand) for both contact printing and enlarging.

Photometers in Printing and Enlarging

It is my personal opinion that the habitual use of a photometer in printing or enlarging may invalidate expressive controls. However, from a purely mechanistic point of view, a photometer can indicate the opacity range of a negative, and the proper contrast grade of paper required. Also, the range of intensities of the image on the enlarging easel may be measured—either a broad average, or the values of specific areas. The photometer readings can be interpreted in terms of the print or the enlargement. But, as is shown elsewhere, the important qualities of a print or an enlargement are subjective. Only by a sensitive appraisal of subtle values can an expressive print be made. As was stated on page 21, we should first print for the lighter values of the image. When we have approximated the desired values of the near-whites, we turn our attention to the darker values, and achieve the required depth and relationship of tones chiefly by modification of the developer. As in basing the exposure of a negative on average exposure-meter readings and without visualization, the use of a photometer to determine print values may give results that are not fully expressive.

No matter how extensively he uses a photometer in printing, a photographer will always have to *look* at his prints and judge them subjectively and emotionally—unless he will be satisfied with a mere mechanical reproduction. Purely mechanical measurements are of course very helpful for study and controls, but are not essential in making an expressive print. An old adage in music is equally applicable in photography: "If you play when you practice, you will practice when you play."

The reader must not think that I do not favor the frequent objective analysis of negatives and prints. My plea is not to confuse the expressive with the mechanical. The Weston Fotoval is an excellent instrument for on-easel evaluation of negatives and I believe any serious photographer should own such an instrument, and use it intelligently in the control of his technique. Further discussion of the use of this instrument will be found on page 22.

19. Colonial Doorway, New Jersey. A problem of luminous whites and shadows.

PROCESSING THE PRINT

In theory, the process of development (the chemical reduction of silver halide) is practically alike for negatives and developing-out papers. In both, an invisible latent image is produced by exposure to light and subsequently revealed by development. In both, the image is expressed as a deposit of reduced metallic silver. In both, we may apply controls to achieve desired effects. These controls, however, are not necessarily alike.

Whereas exposure determines the potential range of opacities in a negative—and hence the brilliancies in the print made from it—the range actually attained is determined by the development of that negative. Thus the relationship between the range of brightnesses in the subject and the range of brilliancies in the ultimate print depends upon the exposure of the negative and the degree to which the negative is developed, as well as upon the choice of printing paper and the handling of the print. Values in the print may suggest either reality or departure from reality, depending on the photographer's creative concept. The negative itself has no direct esthetic value.

Various developing procedures may produce certain special effects in the negative, but such effects are meaningless unless they intentionally relate to the making of the print. A negative may have a bluish or a brownish tone, be hard or flat, thin or dense; but these qualities have no emotional significance in themselves and do not necessarily affect the print. There is no such thing as a "perfect" negative in terms of arbitrary ideal values. A negative is but a means to an end—which is the final print.

Development of the print or the enlargement involves many more effects than the mere degree of reduction of silver. There are various developing agents, and many of these in various concentrations and combinations yield different contrasts and different colors of image on a given paper. Hence the proper selection and application of a print developer are of the greatest importance. Time of development, temperature, and degree of exhaustion of the developer solution have profound effects on the quality of the print.

The photographer must recognize how great an effective range of values and tones he can control in printing, and should learn to select that combination of factors which best suits his purpose. The fact that many papers and developing procedures of today are designed to give warm olive-black tones should in no way influence the photographer who may desire something different. He may choose his print developer to suit the subject (not only the paper); the subtle tonal color of a print profoundly influences its emotional effect. (By "print color" I mean merely a trend toward greenish, bluish, or brownish tones in the black-and-white image. A fully toned print, in which a definite *color* appears, is something entirely different.)

The important characteristics of a good print developer include:

1. *Efficient total reduction* of the exposed silver halide, with minimum fog. Although in a negative a certain amount of allover fog may be present without deleterious effect, in print emulsions fog degrades the lighter values and thus destroys the vitality of the image. (See page 116 for a special bleaching formula to remove fog after development, and page 60 for antifog treatment.)

2. *A satisfactory color of image.* A discussion of print color from an esthetic point of view is found on page 24. It should be noted here, however, that the effects of print color due to characteristics of the paper and the developer are not easy to explain theoretically, although frequently they are adequately controlled in practice. The color of a print image depends largely on grain size in the developed emulsion. Grain size is affected by the character of the emulsion; the concentration of oxidation products in the developer; the amount of bromide in the emulsion and in the developer solution; the composition, degree of exhaustion, and temperature of the solution; and the time of development. In addition, paper emulsions change progressively in speed, color, and other characteristics through age, poor storage conditions, etc. Further, as is seen on page 42, reciprocity failure must not be discounted in the exposure of prints and enlargements.

Lest he be confused by these numerous and complicated factors, the photographer should either follow at first the formulas and procedures advised by the manufacturer, or (if he intends to pursue the general approach outlined in this book) begin with the procedures outlined on page 60. Once he has established a norm, he may experiment with certain variations to achieve interpretative effects. Personal objectives of quality and effect are of supreme importance in photographic printing; there are subtle emotional and psychological interrelations between tonalities, contrast, print color, and surface effects that cannot be fully evaluated in practical terms or described in a textbook.

Ingredients of Print Developers

The two most extensively used developing agents are:

1. *Metol* (a trade name; other trade names for this chemical include Elon, Pictol, Veritol, etc.). Used as a single agent, it produces a soft and delicate image of good color. It is ordinarily used in conjunction with hydroquinone.

2. *Hydroquinone.* This is one of the first developing agents known. Hydroquinone has the property of enhancing contrast in the image by building up heavier deposits in the shadow areas of a print than could be obtained—in the same development time and from the same exposure—by the use of Metol alone. Hydroquinone and Metol in combination comprise the most popular and most universally used formulas. The formulas give thoroughly consistent results and have the advantages of long life and economy (see pages 112-13).

Most standard print-developer formulas also contain the following chemicals:

3. *Sodium sulfite.** A salt which acts as an antioxidizing agent, thereby prolonging the effective life of the developing agents in the solution. It also acts as a silver solvent, this action being chemically complex but affecting print quality.

---

* Sodium *sulfite* (not sodium *sulfate* or *sulfide*) is prepared in two forms: crystalline and anhydrous (desiccated). Their relative strengths are approximately 1:2; in other words twice the amount of crystalline sulfite is required in comparison to anhydrous. In this country it is universally accepted that when sodium sulfite is listed in a formula, the anhydrous (desiccated) form is intended.

4. *Sodium carbonate.** This chemical alkalizes the developer solution. All developing agents (except Amidol) require a definite alkaline environment for their activation. Sodium carbonate is the ingredient most frequently used as an alkalizer, since it is the most efficient and economical for use in print developers.

RELATIVE STRENGTH OF THE THREE FORMS OF SODIUM CARBONATE

Crystal	*Monohydrated*	*Desiccated or Anhydrous*
2.31 parts	1.00 part	.85 parts
2.70 parts	1.17 parts	1.00 part
1.00 part	.43 parts	.37 parts

Use 17% more monohydrated than desiccated to equal strength. Use 15% less desiccated than monohydrated to equal strength. Refer to PHOTO-LAB-INDEX Section 12, p. 7, for conversion tables.

5. *Potassium bromide.* An important ingredient of most developers. In popular concept potassium bromide "prevents fog." What it actually does in developers should be better understood by all photographers. Any photographic emulsion has a tendency to pass automatically from an unexposed-halide state to a developable state, and that tendency is augmented by age, dampness, and other damaging influences. During development of the image there is a tendency for the developer to reduce some unstable *unexposed* halide as well as exposed halide. The presence of a sufficient amount of bromide in the developer inhibits this erratic reduction of the unexposed grains, and fog is thereby minimized. If more bromide is added than the amount required to prevent fog, the general depression of emulsion speed that results is more evident in the lighter portions of the image, and contrast is effectively increased. The addition of still greater amounts of bromide, however, results in a restraining action on all parts of the image. Perhaps the chief disadvantage of the presence of excess bromide in the developer is the production of greenish-black tones. A powerful restraining effect may be produced without the disadvantage of greenish-black tones by the use of antifoggants.

6. *Antifoggants* have lately become justifiably popular. Certain chemicals such as benzotriazole, 6-nitrobenzimidazole nitrate, and some proprietary products such as Kodak Antifog, BB compound, Halodol, etc., are specified in developers as restrainers in addition to or in replacement of potassium bromide. They act in about the same way as potassium bromide, but yield better tones and prolong the life of the solution. Used with papers that favor warm tones, they will definitely cool those tones, thereby giving the photographer a wide range of control of print color.

Standard Metol-hydroquinone (and other) formulas, as recommended by the manufacturers for use with their products, vary in several particulars. Each manufacturer designs formulas balanced for a particular paper emulsion to gain a particular effect. It is presumptuous for the practicing photographer to suppose that he can improve on the carefully planned formulas designed to give standard

---

* Sodium carbonate is obtainable in three forms: crystalline, monohydrated, and anhydrous (desiccated). Relative activities of these three forms are given in the table above. Note that in most formulas the monohydrated (mono.) or anhydrous (anh.) (desiccated—des.) salt is indicated, and if any form other than the one listed is used the amount *must* be converted to equivalent strength.

20. Winery Interior, Lodi, California. A subject of extreme contrast. Negative processed normally, hence of relatively high contrast. Print on Kodabromide No. 1, developed in Amidol diluted 1:15. While this shows the excellent control possible with Amidol in weak dilutions, it must be said that the negative should have been properly processed in the first place. Yet every photographer will be confronted with negatives of this type, and it is helpful to know how to manage them. Water-bath development, two-solution developers, or the Pyrocatechin Compensating formula (see Book 2), would have yielded a far better negative. Two flashlamps (hidden at right) and one flashlamp at the camera provided the lighting. The tanks were of very dark wood and the filter apparatus was painted with bright aluminum.

effects. Of course a creative person is not satisfied with standard effects, but he must have a sound point of departure, lest he grope in an experimental morass.

One of the most noticeable differences between standard formulas (as recommended by manufacturers) is the variation in the amount of bromide indicated per volume of solution. The amount of bromide required in a developer depends upon the constitution of the emulsion to which it is to be applied and on the reduction potential of the developing agent used,* also on the concentration in the developing solution of that agent and of the alkali content. We may vary the amount of restrainer to meet special requirements. For example, in using a variable-contrast developer such as the Beers Two-Solution Formula, it is best to mix the solutions without potassium bromide, and to add this or another restrainer as required. A means of determining the minimum amount of restrainer required in any solution to prevent fog on any paper is given on page 61.

In addition to the standard Metol-hydroquinone developers there are other developer agents that give excellent results. Two among these are:

7. *Amidol*, which produces rich strong black tones, slightly on the cold side, preferred by many for its flexibility and the consistency of tone produced in either concentrated or extremely diluted solutions. Its chief disadvantages are that it must be mixed just before use (as it deteriorates rapidly), and it stains fingers and fabrics severely. This developer agent has the unusual property of reducing silver halides without the presence of an alkali in its solution; the ordinary Amidol formulas contain only Amidol, sodium sulfite, and potassium bromide. Occasionally a small amount of citric acid is added to maintain the optimum pH (acidity or alkalinity) of the solution.**

An Amidol solution is easy to prepare, since the proportions of Amidol and sulfite need not be exact. Concentrated standard solutions of sodium sulfite and of potassium bromide can be prepared as stock and then diluted when needed. The Amidol should not be added until the time of use.

Progressively softer results are obtained by diluting the Amidol solution; I have diluted the standard formula (page 112) with up to 20 times its volume of water and achieved prints of beautiful tone from negatives of extreme contrast. Developing time, however, was very long—10 minutes and more. In normal concentration, Amidol solutions can be used with alternate immersion of the print (without agitation) in plain water. This water-bath treatment gives full development of the light values of the print, but holds back development of the deeper tones (see Book 2, p. 104). The print color is quite good—at the end of the alternate baths the print can be placed in the developer for a short time to build the blacks to the desired depth of tone.

---

* The term "reduction potential" appears frequently in photographic literature. It is a poorly understood expression, used with the same casualness as is the term "gamma." A developing agent is said to have a high reduction potential if it is relatively unaffected by the presence of bromide in the solution or in the emulsion. Hydroquinone has been given the arbitrary reduction potential of 1, Metol that of 20, Amidol that of 35 plus.

**Sodium sulfite reacts with water to produce a mild alkaline effect. The citric acid is a weak acid and serves to maintain the pH at the appropriate level, thus inhibiting the discoloration of the solution and the staining of the print that results when an Amidol solution becomes too alkaline.

8. *Glycin*, usually used in conjunction with Metol or hydroquinone, or both, as a paper developer. It gives rich, brilliant images, and—in suitable combination with other ingredients—produces a variety of print colors. Usually a slow-working developer, it is recommended when a considerable number of prints are to be developed at one time (see Mass Production of Prints, page 99).

Formulas employing other agents, and listings of proprietary developers, may be found in other textbooks and in manufacturers' handbooks.

The action of a developer solution responds, as does almost any chemical reaction, to temperature change. Raising the temperature makes the action more rapid, so that less time is required for full development; lowering the temperature retards the action, so that more time is required to achieve the normal effect. We can consider 68° F as the normal temperature for normal results. This particular temperature has been selected as the most efficient for a variety of reasons, including practical developing time, efficiency of the solutions, and consistent print color and contrast. For the most stable results, developer, stop bath, fixing baths, and wash water should be as near to this same temperature as practicable. At times when conditions are not controllable, or when we desire certain altered effects, the temperature of the developer may be higher or lower than the norm. The extent of the change of activity due to temperature change is represented by the temperature coefficient for the developing agent.

In a formula containing only one developing agent, the temperature coefficient and the required change in developing time are easily determined. But in a developer that contains two or more agents, each with a different temperature coefficient, it is more practical to experiment than to compute. Not only is the time of development affected by change of temperature, but the character of the developer is also changed, so that the print quality is altered. For example, although the action of Metol is consistent over a wide range of temperatures (the required developing time varying uniformly with temperature change), the action of hydroquinone is somewhat irregularly affected by variations in temperature. Hydroquinone loses much activity at 55° F but has a very high activity at or above 75° F.* Consequently the Metol-hydroquinone developer, producing normal effects at 68° F, gives somewhat softer effects as the temperature is lowered (and the activity of the hydroquinone is thereby diminished), and more vigorous effects as the temperature is raised (and the activity of the hydroquinone is increased). Roughly speaking, a cold Metol-hydroquinone developer acts as though it were mostly Metol. A certain amount of control is thus possible through variations in the temperature of a Metol-hydroquinone developer; but results should be evaluated on the basis of print color as well as contrast.

It should be recognized that standard formulas are designed not only to produce desired print quality, but also to balance a number of other requirements.

At times, however, the balanced formulas may not give desired special effects, and modifications of the formulas and of the recommended development times may be required to produce the desired contrast and print color. For example, an Amidol developer may be used at high concentration and at a fairly high temperature (75° F) to give an extremely rich and brilliant print. (The disadvantage is that this solution is short-lived and fairly expensive.) The optimum

---

* Recent investigations indicate that hydroquinone will retain activity at lower temperatures than it is popularly supposed to.

21. Church, San Francisco. The values of the façade were placed on Zone VI, the sky on Zone IV. Normal-plus-plus development was given. (The negative was exposed with an X-1 filter.) The reflection of the sun on the crosses was extremely bright, and prints pure white (Zone IX). Varying degrees of "printing down" would still show the crosses as pure white. In the original print the values are defined more clearly than in the reproduction.

developer formulas meet requirements other than standard image qualities; these requirements must be evaluated by the individual photographer in terms of his own work. There is unfortunate emphasis on speed in processing; speed, however, may be justifiable for quantity production. It should not be applied to creative work, lest it foster a restless impatient attitude incompatible with careful and contemplative photography.

Agitation

As in negative development, agitation of the print in the developer is a most important factor. Not only does adequate agitation prevent streaks and uneven development, but it also keeps the print contrast consistent—from test to print, and from one print to another. As is seen elsewhere, if after partial development a print is allowed to rest in the developer without agitation, the results are softer; that is, the lighter values receive proportionally more development than the deeper values. Figure 22 is a normal print. Figures 23a and 23b show the effects of water-bath and static development.

22. New York City. From a negative made with a Zeiss-Ikon Super Ikonta B camera. The apparent distortion of the vertical lines could have been overcome by tilting the enlarging easel. See the Photo-Lab Index, Sec. 17, pp. 31-32, for a fine description of practical variography. This is a normal full-scale print, developed 3 minutes in Beers No. 5, and should be compared to Figs. 23 a-b and 29 a-b.

23a. Effect of Water-Bath Development. With slightly more exposure, tones are smoother and richer than in Fig. 22. (Whites have more definition.)

23b. Effect of Static Development. Print was allowed to stand in the developer without agitation for 3 minutes after appearance of the image.

Stop Bath

When the image has been developed sufficiently, the print should be removed from the developer and immersed directly in a stop bath, which arrests development by neutralizing the alkalinity of the developing solution remaining in the emulsion and in the paper base. The commonest stop-bath solution is very dilute acetic acid (see formula, page 115). If the print were to be placed directly in the fixing bath—without treatment in the stop bath—development might be unevenly arrested, permitting production of stains, and the fixing bath would be harmed by developer chemicals carried over on the print. It is poor economy to use an exhausted stop bath.

Fixing Bath

The function of a fixing bath is to make the image permanent by removing all the unexposed and undeveloped silver halide that remains in the emulsion after development, and without affecting the exposed and developed silver grains. The most practical fixative is sodium thiosulfate (popular name, "hypo," a contraction of "hyposulfite," which is an erroneous term).

A fixing bath usually contains several other ingredients. Those used in addition to the hypo are (in the order of mixing):

1. *Sodium sulfite,* a preservative, to prevent the decomposition of the hypo solution that may be caused by contact with acid.

2. *Acetic acid,* which produces the acidity required for the most efficient action of the bath (a pH of 5.6), and counteracts the alkalinity of any developer solution the stop bath has not neutralized.

3. *Boric acid,* a buffer to maintain the proper acidity of the bath during its effective life, and to prevent sludging.

4. *Potassium alum,* to harden the emulsion, and thus prevent the blistering and frilling that may be caused by acid solutions and warm wash water, and to prevent simple physical damage during washing.

Variations on or departures from the standard formulas may include Kodalk, potassium-chrome alum, sulfuric acid, potassium metabisulfite, etc., but for the most part they have little practical advantage over the standard formulas. A possible exception is a simple formula in which potassium metabisulfite (or sodium bisulfite) is added to the hypo (page 115); some workers believe this formula gives a slightly better color to the final print, although, lacking a hardener, it can be used only in cool weather or when the temperature of the wash water is not above 68° F.

Solutions of sodium thiosulfate alone may be used for fixing, provided the print is treated in a fresh stop bath and thoroughly rinsed in water before fixation. Since some acid is certain to be carried over into the plain hypo bath, resulting in precipitation of sulfur, the useful life of this plain fixing bath is short.*

The use of two or three fixing baths in sequence, as described on page 103, is recommended for maximum permanence of the prints. Bath number 1 should be the regular acid fixing bath (a formula such as Kodak F-5), and, if the wash water does not exceed 68° F, the following baths may be of plain hypo. When the number 1 bath is discarded, the number 2 bath (with the addition of acid hardener if required) takes its place, and a new number 2 or number 3 bath is prepared. The principle of the sequence of baths is this: The first bath clears and fixes the print (that is, removes practically all the unexposed and undeveloped silver halides). But as a fixing bath is used, an accumulation of silver salts appears in the solution, and these salts are redeposited on the print. Being inert, they are difficult if not impossible to remove by washing. The function of the second bath is to remove these deleterious salts, and the function of the third bath is to assure permanency by further removal of injurious compounds from the print. In general practice, I give the first fixation, then soak the prints in circulating water until the printing session is completed, then pass all prints through a fresh plain hypo bath (an acid hardener fixing bath if the wash water is over 68° F). The first bath is capable of fixing a great number of prints, but the greater the number of prints fixed, the more dangerous the accumulation of the inert salts, and the more necessary the second bath.

The time of fixation has been recently subject to revision. The old rule for negatives was to "fix for twice as long as it takes to clear." Prints clear rapidly— as you can observe by placing a developed print in the fixing bath under a good light. A print may be fixed in 2 minutes (in an ordinary bath) if it is constantly agitated and the solution flows continuously over the entire surface of the print. In practical use, it takes somewhat longer to fix a print adequately, perhaps 4 minutes if several prints are in the solution at one time. Hence, 3 or 4 minutes in the first bath, and 2 minutes each in the second and third bath, is entirely adequate—provided the baths are correctly compounded and the prints are well agitated during the fixation. Prolonged fixing is almost as detrimental to permanence as insufficient fixing (apparently there are formed near the silver grains sulfide nuclei that will eventually cause fading and change of print color). Also, if fixing is inadequate—being too short or inert salts being allowed to remain in the emulsion—impermanence is assured. Also, it appears that selenium toning will then affect the whites of the image, producing an allover yellowish tone. The same

---

* In mixing acid fixing baths, it is very important that the sulfite be added *before* the acid; otherwise sulfur is precipitated and the fixing bath is ruined.

applies to prolonged fixation—the selenium is apparently attracted by the inert salts that are deposited over the surface (and sometimes also on the back) of the print. "Quick-fixing" solutions for prints I do not think are advantageous. There is danger of dichroic fog appearing unless the stop-bath immersion is adequate.

Hypo Eliminator

Now available in prepared form by several manufacturers, the hypo-eliminator solutions shorten washing time and assure permanence of image. Follow the instructions for use as they appear on the packages. Fresh fixing baths are advisable as described above. (The addition of selenium toner to the hypo-eliminator solution is described on page 116.) After treatment in hypo-eliminator solution and short wash, warm-toned prints may be "cooled" in tone by immersion in the Gold-Protective solution on page 115.

Washing

Washing involves the removal of the fixing chemicals and their residuals, and is one of the most important phases of the entire process. Water for washing should be reasonably pure; vegetable matter and ordinary mineral sludge are not harmful, provided pure water is used to rinse the print off, front and back, before it is swabbed with a clean cloth, cotton, or viscose sponge, and then rinsed again before drying. However, the use of water containing rust, or any dissolved substances that could react with the photographic chemicals, may seriously stain the prints. Rust is especially harmful to prints that are to be toned, producing permanent spots in the image.

Prints require longer washing than negatives because the fixing chemical adheres tenaciously to the paper stock. Some modern papers have a waterproof base, which materially decreases the required washing time, but it must be emphasized that unless washing is adequate, and every part of the print is thoroughly free of the fixing chemicals and their residuals, the print in time will fade or discolor. Merely placing prints in a tray with water running in one side and out the other, but without constant agitation, invites disaster. Although it is possible to wash prints by transferring them from one tray of fresh water to another, treatment of this type cannot give reasonable assurance of permanency without many changes in relatively large amounts of water with constant agitation and considerable time allowed in each change of water.

Draining and Swabbing

To one side of the washing sink or tray (preferably to the right) there should be an inclined surface of glass, stainless steel, or the bottom of a clean, noncorroded tray on which the prints are placed in order to drain following washing. Obviously, if most of the water is drained off before the prints are laid out to dry, the prints will dry faster and be less subject to damage from water drops gathering on their surfaces. However, the print should be swabbed off before drying—the surface always, and the back as well if there is any chance that there are inert impurities in the wash water.

If only the face of the print is to be swabbed, I advise the following procedure: While applying a gentle stream of water from a flexible hose to the face of the print, swab off every part with a clean viscose sponge. Then squeeze the sponge out and remove excess surface water. Then lay the print face down to dry (as described below). If there is a considerable number of prints, they can be swabbed off and placed, one after the other, on another draining surface.

Then, just before they are laid out to dry, the excess moisture can be removed with the viscose sponge. This assumes that the back of the print is clean; if it is not, it will affect the surface of the print lying under it.

If both face and back are to be swabbed I suggest the following: First lay the prints on the draining surface face down and allow them to drain. Then swab the back of the print first (as above), remove it from the pile, and place it face up on another draining board. Swab the face thoroughly (as above). Then proceed with the next print, and so on down through the pile. Then, as described in the paragraph above, remove excess moisture from the print face before laying it out to dry. It is obvious that the procedure outlined above is designed to prevent transmission of any gross impurities from the face of one print to the back of another, or vice versa.

Drying

I do not speak here about mechanical dryers, ferrotyping, etc., as I am seldom interested in the production of high-gloss ferrotyped surfaces. I have found that a perfectly satisfactory method of drying prints consists of placing the print face down on a *clean* stretched cheesecloth (see Book 1, p. 89). If the excess moisture is removed from the face of the print before it is laid out to dry (and from the back of the print after it is on the cloth), the print will dry evenly and fairly flat. Of course single-weight prints will curl much more than double-weight prints; in a very dry climate, single-weight prints should probably be dried between photo blotters. But these blotters must be very clean, and pressure must not be exerted while prints are drying between them, as the blotter texture may be impressed on the print surface, reducing smoothness. Prints on drying racks can be allowed to dry naturally, or warm air can be directed over them. If there is ample natural circulation of air and the racks are adequately separated (about 3 inches apart), prints should dry overnight in climates of average humidity. See that prints do not overlap or the edges or corners rest over the drying-frame edge. Even if the prints have been most thoroughly washed, the cheesecloth will, in time, accumulate enough residual chemicals from the prints and dust from the air to warrant a change. I suggest that the cloth be cleaned frequently with a vacuum cleaner to remove inevitable dust and lint.

Clearing the Whites

Even slight fog in a print veils the whites and reduces brilliancy and sparkle. This veiling occurs in many modern papers, especially when fully developed in order to yield a rich tonality. To overcome this unfortunate effect the washed and dried print is subjected to treatment in a bleaching solution (page 116). Do not attempt to clear the whites after toning.

Pressing

When the prints are dry they should be placed between clean *smooth* cardboards (be certain no grit lies on prints or cardboards) and subjected to moderate pressure for about 24 hours, if possible. This will flatten the print without damage. Under no circumstances try to flatten a print by drawing a ruler or other straight-edge over it. That is almost certain to produce cracks on a glossy surface, and may very well ruin any other type of surface. If flattening must be done rapidly, the prints can be protected by smooth cardboard and subjected to moderate pressure in a warm dry mounting press. It is very difficult to trim the prints accurately unless they are reasonably flat. Most prints are now ready for mounting (see page 83). However, examination may suggest that some will be improved by toning.

Toning

It is my personal opinion that the only satisfactory way to change the natural color of a print and improve its values is to tone the image very slightly—not to produce an obvious color, but to supplant the original "chemical color," which may be unpleasant. The result of slight toning should be a *suggestion* of cool-purple sepia; I feel that this is the most vital and effective modification of the color of the plain silver image. Although the treatment may have but slight physical effect on the brilliance of the image, it has a profound emotional effect. A well-toned print impresses one as being of considerably greater brilliance than the same image untoned.

Toning involves changes in both chemical structure and size of the silver grain; it is therefore impossible to predict in advance the exact quality of tone that will be obtained with different papers and developers and with various toners. Pure bromide papers have little or no response to selenium toning; chlorobromide papers respond with a rather cool tone; and chloride papers are most responsive, tending to yield the warmest tones. Thus it would be difficult, if not impossible, to achieve consistency of tone throughout a set of prints made on different papers. Further, the degree of development given the print affects the results of toning—a fully developed print usually yields a colder tone than one that has received less development.

Certain toning processes are selective, affecting only the lighter (or in some cases the darker) portions of the image, and giving a result that is known as *split toning*. But the separation of tones is seldom logical. Occasionally, selenium toners give a split-tone effect (by toning at first only the higher or the lower values, leaving the middle values unaffected); this sometimes improves a print, but is more likely to be rather disturbing. Intentional split-toning can be achieved by partial bleaching followed by redevelopment in a sulfide bath, or by slightly reducing the print with a ferricyanide reducer.

Under ordinary circumstances, only a minimum degree of toning is desirable. Occasionally, however, full tones are required. Methods for full toning of a print may be classed as follows:

1. *Toning by direct development.* Certain developing agents, such as Adurol or combinations of hydroquinone and glycin, give brownish tones by direct development. Whether or not these tones are satisfactory must be judged by the photographer himself; I find them usually rather muddy and unpleasant.

2. *The standard sepia toning procedure* (a bleach-and-redevelopment process using sodium sulfide). The resultant tone is a warm sepia. Possible variations are a colder sepia, obtained if the print is fully developed, and a warmer sepia, obtained if the print is slightly underdeveloped; this latter variation, however, may turn out to be very unpleasant, suggesting an egg-yolk yellow of most aggressive quality. Formulas are available in most photographic handbooks.

Another warm sepia toning process involves bleaching and redevelopment in thiorurea (thiocarbamide).

3. *The hypo-alum toning process.* In this the image is sulfided by treatment in a single solution (see PHOTO-LAB-INDEX). This process gives a considerably better tone than the ordinary bleach-and-redevelopment system, but it may also suggest a yellowish sepia.

4. *The Nelson gold-toning process.* This is a very satisfactory single-solution process, yielding a quality of tone that I consider superior to 2 and 3 above (see PHOTO-LAB-INDEX).

5. *Selenium toning.* This process is the simplest of all. The proprietary formulas are entirely adequate, and I prefer the Kodak Selenium Toner (liquid concentrate).

I emphasize the necessity of thorough fixing and washing of a print before toning with this—or any other—formula. Toning changes the simple form of the silver comprising the image; if any silver residuals (normally invisible) remain in the emulsion on the print, they may attract the metallic deposit of selenium, resulting in an unfortunate yellowing of the whites. Should this yellow occur, it sometimes can be cleared by immersion in a bath of dilute sodium sulfite. It is important that prints which are to be toned in selenium be treated for several minutes beforehand in a 2% Kodalk solution to neutralize any inherent acidity.

In any of the first three processes, toning should be carried quite far, lest a split tone (and other unpleasant effects) result. Generally, however, toning with selenium should be only very slight—just enough to remove the inherent unpleasant chemical color of the ordinary paper emulsion; 2 to 5 minutes is usually sufficient, but under certain conditions selenium toning may take much longer.

If the photographer has made a fine rich black-and-white print, a very slight application of such toners as selenium should intensify the values sufficiently; in my opinion, the imposition of any obvious color will only detract from the beauty of the print.

Evaluating the Brilliancy of the Final Print

As described in Book 2, the measurement of density (opacity) of the negative is a rather simple procedure; a good densitometer (such as Weston Fotoval, or the Kodak Color Densitometer) offers direct readings of density either by electronically activated dials or by direct comparison with an illuminated spot. To make direct readings of *reflection density* (print brilliancy) requires a more complicated apparatus. The Eastman Transmission and Reflection Densitometer is equipped to measure reflection density, and devices may be fabricated by mechanically minded persons, but the average photographer will find it difficult to locate (or pay for) a reflection densitometer.

However, I have found that an adequate means of determining reflection can be worked out by any interested photographer, as follows:

Order from Kodak or GAF, two calibrated paper wedges, specifying that they be made on chlorobromide paper. Give one of these wedges a *slight* toning in selenium, and have it recalibrated. Make a black paper tube about 1 foot long. Place the print and the step wedge under a 45° angle of illumination; observing through the black tube, compare the whitest and blackest values of the print with the step wedge. An *approximate* reflection-density value can be determined on a comparison basis by this method.

24. Autumn, Glacier National Park, Montana. Here the juxtaposition of pure whites and solid blacks against a neutral-gray background conveys an impression of brilliancy.

DETAILED DESCRIPTION OF MAKING A PRINT

If we have made the desired negative and the visualization of the print is still fresh in our minds from the moment of the original concept (at or before exposure of the negative), we are not obliged to make any tests to decide what paper contrast is required; our negative is scaled for "No. 2" paper and we can proceed accordingly. (See pages 21 and 23 for description of appraisal of a negative.)

Preparation of a Darkroom

Assuming that the darkroom and its equipment are clean and in good working order, our first task is to assemble the necessary equipment and prepare solutions for use. As we are to make a contact print, we will require the following equipment in good working order:

Contact printing frame (see Book 1, p. 87). See that the glass is absolutely clean, and that a sheet of thin, soft material (very thin sponge-rubber pad) is at hand.

Contact printing light. Select the proper strength of lamp for the paper to be used. An ordinary slow chloride paper (such as Azo or Convira) requires a 60-watt to 100-watt frosted lamp; a fast chlorobromide or bromide paper (such as Velour Black or Kodabromide or Brovira) requires a 10-watt frosted lamp, or an amber lamp, or a stronger light properly screened by a diffusing material. The distance of the light from the printing frame can be adjusted by a counter-weighted overhead pulley arrangement, or by having the lamp attached to a horizontal rod or some other support that can be secured in a variety of positions in a vertical track (or vertical sequence of holes) placed above and at the back of the worktable (Fig. 14, page 32).

If fast papers are being used and a vertical enlarger is to provide contact-printing illumination, set the enlarging lens at full aperture and see that masks, negative, and glasses are removed from the negative holder, that the enlarger is raised high enough so that the field of illumination amply covers the contact-printing area, and that the lens is so adjusted that the plane of the condenser surface or the diffusing glass is not in focus at the plane of the printing frame. Check by means of meter readings on a white card or by a photometer, to be certain that the field of illumination is consistently bright over all the area of the negative to be printed.

If a printing box is to be used, see that all glasses are very clean, that pilot-light and printing-light lamps are working, and that the switches are in good order.

Solutions. Prepare the following:

Developer. Three trays for three Beers-formula preparations (soft, normal, and hard). See formula, page 114. Prepare the developer with the proper amount of restrainer for the paper used. The solutions, excepting No. 4 (normal), need not be prepared for use until the first test is made.

The stock solution is made up without restrainer or antifoggant because different papers may require different amounts of restrainer. It is therefore necessary to determine by separate test the amount of restrainer required to prevent chemical fog on any given paper if the maximum expected time of development must be exceeded. (Once this amount has been determined for a particular paper and developer, the test need not be repeated.)

The test is as follows: Add 5 cc of 10% potassium bromide or of 0.4% or 1.0% benzotriazole to each liter of working solution. Place a small strip of paper in the solution and agitate it (without the safelight on) for 3 minutes. Bend the strip over to compare the back with the emulsion side; if no fog has appeared, continue up to 4 or 5 minutes. Check for fog again; if fog has appeared, discard the strip. Add 5 cc more restrainer per liter of developing solution and test again for 4 or 5 minutes. If the strip is not clear, add another 5 cc of restrainer and test again. When after 4 or 5 minutes' immersion in the developer—with constant agitation—no fog appears, we can assume there is sufficient restrainer in the developer for the paper being used. More could be added, but the results would be:

    a. An increased greenish tone with excess bromide, or an increased bluish tone with excess antifoggant
    b. A decrease in paper speed with excess of either restrainer
    c. A slight increase of contrast with excess of either restrainer.

If Metol-glycin developer is to be used for quantity printing (page 99), the fog test should be extended to 10 minutes.

Stop bath. Prepare a stop bath according to the formula on page 115. Place the tray containing it to the right of the developer trays (not too close, lest it slop over into the developer).

Fixing baths· Prepare three baths (as described on page 54).

Water bath. Fill an extra tray with water and place it near the developer trays.
    NOTE: If the darkroom sink is not roomy enough for all the above trays, proceed with only one tray for the developer (keeping unused variations of the Beers formula in jugs) and one tray for the fixing bath, but have the washing sink filled with water in which to "store" prints after the first fixing. When the print session is over, the prints can be put through the No. 2 and No. 3 fixing baths and then washed.

Safelights. Check on the proper safelights for the paper to be used; see that the lamps light up and that the safelight glasses are correctly placed in the safelights so that no white light leaks out around them. Also check the working lights —the red lamps or indirect safelights, which will be kept on constantly, and the bright print-viewing light. (Refer to Book 1 for more extensive discussion of these and other items.)

Accessories: Camel's-hair brush; timer (preferably electric metronome); dodging and burning devices (see page 67); cover card for developing tray; tongs or gloves; apron; small pocket flashlight with red or amber glass (to look for things in the darkroom or to read the stop markings on the enlarger lens); light-tight paper boxes (or see that the lighttight paper drawer is ready for use); hand towels; focusing magnifier; photometer (connected to current); crock of water in sink for rinsing hands.

PRECAUTIONS: See that all doors and windows are tightly closed; that ventilation is working; that no possibility of electric short or shock exists, and that all working notes are at hand.

Now that darkroom and equipment and solutions are ready, we can proceed. The negative is taken from its envelope, placed on the viewer, and inspected for blemishes (which may need spotting). This is the time for a final check on values and for confirmation of the original visualization of the desired print. Then:

The glass of the printing frame and the negative are carefully dusted off, and the negative is placed in the frame with the emulsion side up (the back of the negative resting on the glass). A sheet of printing paper as large as the negative is placed in the frame—emulsion side of paper against emulsion side of negative —the thin pad is placed over the paper, and the frame back is closed.

The timer or metronome is turned on. (For the metronome I suggest a setting of 100 beats a minute; 120 beats a minute would be an interval of $\frac{1}{2}$ second, which some workers may prefer.) The timer, being a variation of an ordinary clock, indicates seconds or fractions thereof. I personally find it much easier to time my printing exposure audibly; I can devote all my visual attention to necessary dodging and burning without need for frequent glancing at the clock.

The frame is turned over and placed under the light. A cardboard larger than the area of the negative is laid over the printing frame, and the light is turned on. A timing rhythm is established, and the card is quickly and completely removed.

Now, with a little experience, the approximate exposure can be judged, and the sequence of a few test exposures will include the final desired exposure. But in the beginning we may have to make a few bold experiments with $\frac{1}{2}$-inch test strips before we arrive at an approximate correct exposure. Let us assume that we have made such a rough preliminary test, and we know the exposure is somewhere around 15 seconds. Our object will be to adjust our light for an exposure somewhere between 15 and 25 seconds; in less than 15 seconds we will not have adequate control, but more than 60 seconds' exposure may introduce a reciprocity-departure effect that alters the effective exposure scale of the paper. Therefore we will assume that the exposure is around 20 seconds. If our metronome is set on seconds, we will count 20; on $\frac{1}{2}$ seconds we count 40; on 100 beats per minute we count 33. In counting, we start with 0 ("0, 1, 2, 3 . . .").

As we are to print first for the lightest values in the subject, we will seek a place in the negative large enough to allow a group of exposures to be given; let us select the white shirt in Figure 25; it is a large enough area to permit examination of 5 different degrees of exposure. We will "bracket" our test exposures as follows:

20, 25, 30, 35, 40 (at 100 beats per minute) or

24, 30, 36, 42, 48 (at $\frac{1}{2}$-second intervals—120 beats per minute)

Throughout the following example, let us use the 100 beats per minute. We make the test in this way:

1. Turn the light on, and on the first beat (which we count as "0"), quickly remove the covering cardboard.

2. At beat 20 quickly move the card over 1/5 of the light area.

3. At beat 25 quickly move the card over another 1/5 of the area.

4. At beat 30 move the card over an additional 1/5 of the area.

5. At beat 35 move the card over an additional 1/5 of the area.

6. Allow the last 1/5 of the area to have the final 5 beats' exposure.

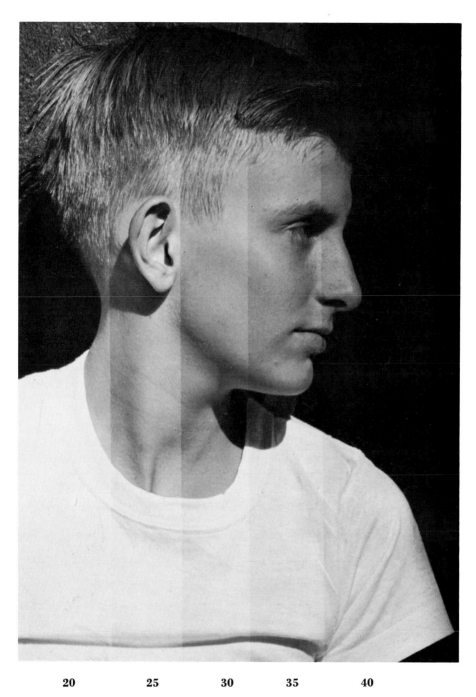

20	**25**	**30**	**35**	**40**

25. Illustrating a Typical Test Print. The print is divided roughly into 5 sections; the units of exposure each has received are given below the strips. Refer to text on pages 62, 64-65, for full description. Full-scale tests of this type are more economical (especially of time) than many small test strips, and by showing the effects of varying exposures on different parts of the image, they suggest what dodging and burning may be required.

Open the frame, remove the paper, and immerse it quickly and evenly in the developer. This should be Beers No. 4 (normal) adjusted to 68° F temperature.* Develop for 3 minutes, with constant agitation. Place it in the stop bath for 30 seconds, then in the fixing bath; after 30 seconds, examine the test print under a bright light.

If no variation of tone appears in the light area, it is obvious that the exposures have been insufficient, and the test must be made over again—starting from the previous maximum. The increase in exposure need not be gained by increasing the *time*; rather, the intensity of the light can be increased by 1) moving it closer to the negative; 2) keeping it at the same distance but using a globe of twice the power; 3) if an enlarger is used for illumination, moving the assembly closer to the negative or opening the lens to a larger aperture. Here is where a photometer is of real value—to measure the required intensity of the printing light.

With the adjustments of the printing light made, retest as before. Expose and develop in the same way and examine the result. If we have found suitable exposures, we now have 5 different—slightly different—values for the lightest area of the print (white shirt). Which one seems to be most satisfactory? We bend over the corner of the print and compare the pure white of the paper with the whites of the image.** Let us say that the 25-count exposure seems most satisfactory. What we visualized as Zone VIII (see Book 2) appears as a slightly textured white, just about as we visualized it should be. (Never test for pure whites; if they appear less than pure white, the exposure is obviously too great.) We test for Zone VIII values because they represent the effective threshold of emulsions, just as Zone I values, relative to the deepest values in a subject, represent the effective threshold of a negative emulsion.

Now place a piece of paper in the frame and make an exposure identical with the selected test exposure (in this case 25 counts), develop it with constant agitation for 3 minutes, fix it, and examine it under the bright light. We now see the entire image, and the relationship of all other values to the desired value of the lightest part. Let us study this for a moment; perhaps our first impression is that the blacks are not sufficiently rich, and what should be a rich, full black is only a deep gray. Although an average spectator might not recognize this loss of "body" as important, we wish to approach perfection as closely as possible. However, we must remember that the print will "dry down"; some of the brilliance of the wet print will be lost, and all tones will be slightly deeper in value. We can achieve a suggestion of the effect of a dry print by holding the wet one at a sharp angle to the light, tilted so that the face of the print almost goes into shadow. We will note that the lower values then appear deeper, although the lighter values usually remain relatively unchanged.

What is the next step? Our test has been made in Beers No. 4; the indications are for similar exposure (to retain the desired Zone VIII values) but for

---

* It is assumed that we have previously made these fundamental tests: a) for general darkroom illumination to prevent fog; b) for determining the proper amount of restrainer required in the developer for the paper used. (See pages 28 and 60.)

** It is efficient to have a completely fixed (unexposed and undeveloped) piece of paper at hand in the washing tray or tank for purposes of comparison.

development in a more vigorous developer (to intensify the deeper tones). Accordingly, we prepare a sufficient amount of Beers No. 6 (see table, page 114), expose another sheet of paper for 25 counts, and develop for 3 minutes with constant agitation. When it is fixed, we examine the new print and we find that the blacks have now achieved proper depth of tone—they are rich and solid. The lighter values, however, are slightly depressed; the more potent developer has acted on them slightly. Now we use a small test strip to obtain exposures in the light (Zone VIII) area of 22, 23, and 24 counts. We develop this test strip as before in Beers No. 6 and compare the whites with those of the first full-size print. We may find that in this case 23 counts is about right. We then make another test, using a strip across the lightest and the darkest areas; upon development and fixation we find that now both the dark and the light areas are acceptable (although the developing time must be increased slightly—say to $3\frac{1}{2}$ minutes). Why, you may ask, did not the blacks appear lighter with the slightly reduced exposure? It is because the lightest values lie very near the threshold of the paper and respond to a very slight change in exposure. But the blacks approach the maximum density of the paper emulsion, and such a slight reduction of exposure causes only an imperceptible change in their values. The greater activity of the developer (Beers No. 6) brought the blacks to "maturity" more positively than did the Beers No. 4 solution. We might find that No. 5 or No. 7 would be right.

Of course we could have given more exposure in the first place and achieved the desired value in the blacks; but the light values would have been seriously depressed. We could have altered the character of the No. 4 developer by adding more restrainer (potassium bromide or benzotriazole), then giving more exposure; the restrainer would have effectively increased the contrast of the paper and might have preserved the desired qualities in the lightest tones while allowing the blacks to reach a deeper value. However, print color would be affected if potassium bromide were added, the prints taking on a greenish quality. In these tests we have developed to the practical maximum; further development would depress the light tones (see page 14 for explanation of the effects of prolonged development), and further prolonged development would result in fog.

Hence it appears that Beers No. 6 is the logical developer for this print. We now make a print, exposing for 23 counts, and developing in Beers 6 for $3\frac{1}{2}$ minutes with constant agitation, neutralizing in the stop bath for 30 seconds, and fixing for 1 minute before examination. All the values are now approximately correct; we have completed our exposure-development control and the print can now be appraised for possibly needed expressive controls—such as dodging or burning—to intensify the photographic concept. We now write on the negative envelope a description of the paper used, the strength of the printing light and its distance from the frame, the exposure given (we can use the symbol 23/100 for 23 100-per-minute counts), the developer used, and the developing time. At first reading this procedure might appear to be exceptionally complicated. In fact, it soon becomes "second nature" to approach printing in this way.

The first point to observe is the "edge effect." When we lay the print on a white surface, (representing the final mount) we will probably notice that the edges appear to be slightly weak in tone. Greater exposure is needed at the edges of the print than in the central areas. To indicate this, we draw a rectangle on the negative envelope and in it (or next to it, if we prefer) we draw a symbol: (#6—page 70) and write next to it 3/100. This means that the print is to get an additional progressive exposure of 3 counts from center to edge. My usual method of accomplishing this is to draw a cardboard across the print, toward the center from the sides of the print (or moved out to the sides from the center). This gives the desired increase of exposure to all sides, but it is obvious that each corner receives twice the exposure of the sides. See Figure 27b.

If this edge-burning requires 3 counts or more, it can be accomplished by using a square dodging card several inches across that, with constant horizontal motion, is brought down within the time required from near the light (where its shadow completely covers the print) to a point very close to the print. My symbol for this is (#9 on page 70). (See Fig. 27a). My experience indicates that practically every print requires some burning of the edges, especially prints that are to be mounted on a white card, as the flare from the card tends to weaken visually the tonality of the adjacent areas. Edge-burning must never be overdone; one should never be aware that it has been done. Its effect is to unify the general tonal values. Occasionally when a critical light area lies along the edge of the print, the additional exposure of the edge-burning may be too apparent. In such cases the light area should be dodged during the main exposure for the same number of counts that is to be given for the edge-burning.

We now appraise the print to see if there are any particular areas in which dodging or burning is required.

26a. Golden Gate Bridge. Print without any edge-burning.

26b. Same. Print with moderate edge-burning.

27a

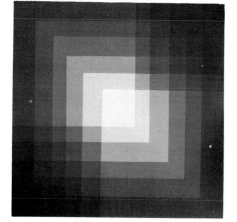

27c

27b

27a. Exaggerated Demonstration of Edge-Burning. Burning progressively to edges by use of a dodging device brought from surface of paper to light source (or vice versa).

27b. Same. Burning progressively to the edges by use of a card moved across the entire width of the paper from *center to edge* (or vice versa), and so applied to all 4 edges. Note darkening of corners obtained by this method.

27c. Same. Burning progressively to the edges by use of a card moved from *center to corner* (or vice versa), and repeated to the opposite corner. Note 2 heavy and 2 light corners.

Burning and Dodging Equipment

For *burning* large areas of the print (that is, adding more exposure locally to the print or enlargement), an ordinary flexible card is best. This card can be bent, and then tilted at an angle to the plane of the paper, producing a curved shadow line that may at times be useful. For burning small areas, holes of different size and shape can be cut into a card, and these openings held over the desired areas of the print.

For *dodging* (that is, withholding exposure locally from the print or enlargement), a flexible card (same as above) is adequate for controlling large areas. For small areas, pieces of opaque card or plastic, cut to different size and shape and attached to a firm but small gauge wire, are adequate.

It is important that all dodging or burning be carried out with constant movement of the devices; otherwise the effects will show on the print.

Dodging and burning kits can be purchased, but I am sure the photographer will find he can prepare his own devices, scaled and shaped to his requirements.

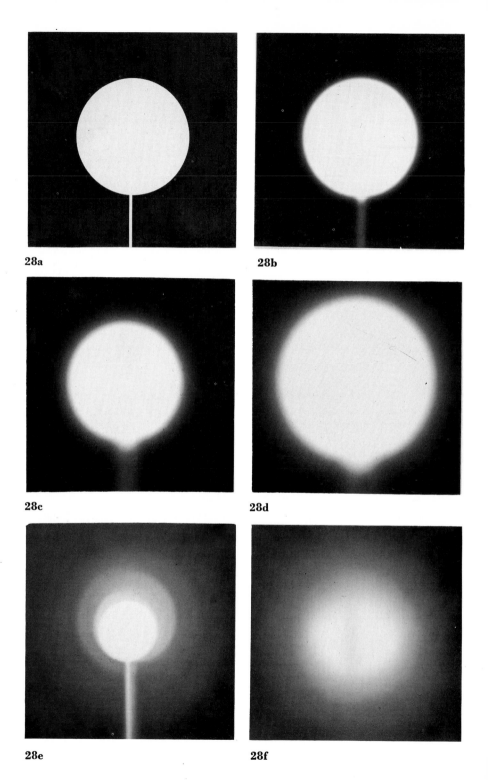

28a

28b

28c

28d

28e

28f

29a. Same as Fig. 22. Showing careless, unequal shading (dodging) of the left-hand side of the image.

29b. Same as Fig. 22. Showing careless, unequal burning of the upper-left sky area.

28a-f. Showing Shadow Effects with Dodgers Held at Various Distances above the Print. Semi-condenser enlarger with a 4″ lens used at 18″ from the paper.

28a. Shadow of 50¢ Piece on Wire Resting on Paper. Shadow sharp—all umbra.

28b. Shadow of 50¢ Piece Held a Few Inches above Paper. Shadow mostly umbra, but some penumbra showing.

28c. Shadow of 1¢ Coin Held Midway between Paper and Lens. Penumbra more marked.

28d. Shadow of 1¢ Coin Held Quite Close to Lens. More penumbra than in 28c.

28e. Insufficient or Too Similar Motion of Dodger during Exposure. Shown by relatively sharp spiral shadows. These would show in any continuous-tone area of the print.

28f. Dodger Kept in Constant, Dissimilar, Motion. Penumbra quite diffuse. For edge-burning, a larger dodger in relation to print size should be used—or bring the dodger closer to the light. Of course the closer the dodger to the light, and the more extensive the penumbra, the more the general illumination of the print will be reduced. Hence dodging with a large dodger close to the paper will not affect undodged areas; dodging with a small dodger close to the light may considerably affect undodged areas, giving the appearance of reduced general exposure.

NOTE: The above examples were made with semicollimated light from an enlarger; with diffuse light sources, the shadow will be much more diffused—that is, the penumbra will be much more apparent at any distance from the paper. If we supplant the opaque dodger with an opening of the same size in an opaque board we shall get an area of illumination instead of an area of shadow, and the process is then termed "burning." As the effects are the same (in reverse), there is no need to demonstrate them here.

The symbols described below are my personal devices to record the various forms of dodging and burning as applied to printing and enlarging. Every photographer can work out his own symbols; these serve only as suggestions.

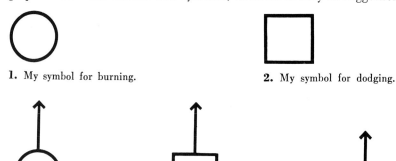

1. My symbol for burning.

2. My symbol for dodging.

3
4
5

3. Directional symbol for burning.
4. Directional symbol for dodging.
5. Begin dodging or burning from this line, point, or area of the picture.

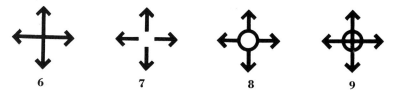

6
7
8
9

6. Edge-burning from center to each edge.
7. Edge-burning from edge towards center.
8. Edge-burning to each corner (or from corner to center).
9. Edge-burning from center to all corners at once (or from corners to center).

31. Tioga Lake: Exaggerated Effect of Burning. Bottom, straight test print. Top, print burned according to symbols on the right edge. Burning begins at the point opposite the center of the circle and progresses in direction of the arrow. Progression may be even, or may be increased or retarded, depending on the amount of burning desired. The photographer must remember that these are my own personal symbols; he may be able to develop a more intelligible system of his own. Or he may be content to do without one and work out his control procedures with every new printing of his negatives.

The lower image shows 5 test areas, obtained by moving card to the right every 10 units of exposure. The accumulated exposure is 10 to 50 units. From the test print I determined that the water is best at 20 units. This is, then, the basic exposure, being the shortest (basic) exposure time. The sky is best at 30 units (signifying burning *up* for 10 additional units). The middle foreground is also best at 30 units (signifying burning *down* for 10 additional units), and the lower foreground is best at 40 units (signifying burning *down* for 10 additional units). Or from basic exposure, burning down for 10 to 20 units. In addition, all sides were burned 5 units from about 1″ in toward the edges.

One may well ask: If you know how to expose a negative properly, why all this manipulation with light to gain the desired print? The answer is simply this: This negative yields a perfectly good *literal* print without any burning (except that the edge-burning is always helpful in overcoming camera flare and the psychophysical conflict between the image and the white mount). The burning procedure (exaggerated here to a certain degree) simply provides the photographer with a method of control of the emotional values. If this control produces an obviously "manipulated" effect, the result is of course destructive.

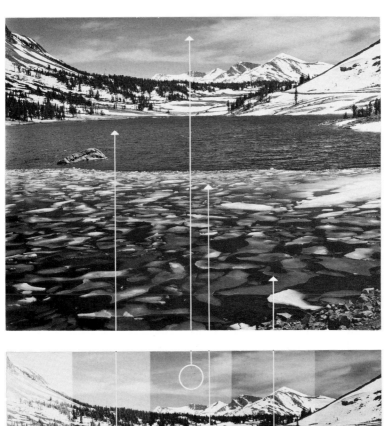

31. Tioga Lake: Exaggerated Effect of Burning.

The gray scale runs from IX (top) down to 0 (bottom), labeled GRAY SCALE | ZONES.

32. Half Dome, Winter, Yosemite Valley. At this point, it is well to recapitulate the basic factors of my approach to photographic technique. Here we have an image combined with a gray scale. Within the limitations of the reproduction process, these relationships are clear. Book 2 describes the relation of zones to brightness values of the subject, density (opacity) values of the negative, and brilliancy values of the print. These relationships, being partly factual and partly emotional, are always subject to *control* variations.

The brightness range of the subject may be slight, or very large. (I have worked with ranges of brightness of 1:2 and 1:4000.) It is impossible to contain the extremes of subject-brightness range within the print; beyond a brilliancy range of 1 to 50 or 60, the relationships must be symbolic. Here is where visualization of the final print at the time of exposure of the negative is of extreme importance. Compensations must be made—not only for factual approximations, but for the emotional transcriptions so necessary to creative photography. We may trust to luck, or we may trust to *reason.* I favor the latter; it pays more creative dividends.

Here we have a typical full-scale image, obviously composed of values relating to Zones I, IV, V, VI, VIII, and IX. (Other zones are represented in the image, but relate to too small areas to show properly in the illustration.) Within the limitations of the halftone process, this picture will give a good idea of the relative values of the subject in terms of zones. The negative was normally exposed and normally developed; the print is on a No. 2 paper, developed in Beers No. 4.

DETAILED DESCRIPTION OF MAKING AN ENLARGEMENT

Prepare the darkroom as described on page 60. Now the enlarger and the enlarging easel will take the place of the contact-printing equipment. First, check the enlarger; see that both inner and outer surfaces of the lens are clean. (Especially in vertical enlargers, the upper surface of the lens may accumulate dust.) Then turn on the light; if a regular condenser enlarger is being used, see that the field of illumination is even. (If the condenser enlargers are of the adjustable type, the light may have to be adjusted for various magnifications.) With diffused-light enlargers we need only check to see if any tubes or lamps have burned out. With mercury-argon (or similar) tube grids, failure of the unit seldom occurs, but if it does, any failure is total. With banks of fluorescent tubes the failure of a single tube will of course result in uneven illumination.

If glass negative carriers are used, see that the glasses are perfectly clean. Glassless carriers are always advised for moderate-sized negatives (4x5 and smaller), but for larger negatives and for critical work, the negative should be supported by two sheets of clear glass clean and free from scratches and bubbles.

It is strongly urged that the enlarger be grounded to prevent accumulation of static charges that would cause dust particles to gather on the negative or the negative-carrier glasses. The interior of the enlarger should be frequently and thoroughly cleaned, preferably with a vacuum cleaner followed by a slightly damp cloth. See that the easel is clean and that the margins and paper guides are properly set. Select the negative; carefully dust it off and place it in the negative carrier so that the emulsion side of the negative faces the lens. Place a piece of white paper on the easel to focus on—a sheet of fixed and washed photo paper with a smooth but not glossy surface is perhaps the best. Any textured paper would make sharp focusing more difficult.

Turn out all but the safelights and turn on the enlarging light. Compose the image on the enlarger easel; when the correct size is achieved, then focus critically at full aperture. A focusing magnifier is of great help. For extremely critical focusing a special lined negative can be used; after the picture size has been determined, remove the negative and replace it with this special-pattern screen. Focus the projected lines to maximum sharpness, and replace the original negative. (Of course this is practical only when glass negative carriers are used and the negative is held perfectly plane. Some glassless carriers have a small strip of focusing negative attached along the edge of the holder. However, I maintain that if a glassless carrier is used, the negative is certain to buckle to some extent, and the image itself should always be carefully examined for maximum sharpness.) In very great enlargements it is impossible to focus the image sharply, as it is not sufficiently sharp itself; maximum sharpness can be obtained by focusing for negative grain. Better still, some small transparent defect in the negative can be used to good advantage. (This problem is discussed further in the section on photomurals, page 104.)

See that the image is sharp all over. If it is sharp along the four edges, we are safe in assuming that the enlarger and the easel are properly aligned. If it is sharp along all edges but unsharp in the center, we can assume that the negative has buckled slightly.

Although we focus first with the lens at full aperture, we may have to stop down to f/16, or even less, to overcome the effects of buckling of the negative. And with some lenses slight refocussing at small apertures may be required. The advantages of a good lens must be emphasized, preferably a coated lens designed specifically for enlarging; with a poor lens all other refinements are futile.

If we have made suitable safelight fog tests, and if the developer has been prepared with the right amount of restrainer for the paper to be used (see page 18), we can proceed with making the enlargement.

We begin by making the tests with the same procedure as outlined in the first example of making a contact print (page 60). Suppose we find upon making the necessary tests that the basic exposure is 30 counts at f/11; we write the following on the negative envelope:

Paper type and grade	Kodabromide F DW 2
Developer	Beers 4 plus 10 cc 10% KBr per liter
Degree of enlargement	1.5 x
Enlarger type	Kodak Precision—diffuse light*
Enlarging lens aperture	f/11
Exposure counts	30/100
Developing time	3 m @ 68° F

Also set down dodging and burning symbols as on page 70.*

Possible Troubles to Watch For

Intensity of enlarging light. Unless a voltage-control device is used, there is always the possibility of changing light intensity, with obviously disconcerting results. Even if the main lines maintain consistent voltage, a sudden drain on the lines (such as turning on electric ranges, etc.) may lower the intensity of the printing or enlarging light. With "cold-light" illuminants, it may require 30 to 60 seconds (sometimes more) for the light to reach maximum brilliancy. Hence such illuminants should be left burning during the entire session of enlarging, not turned on and off for each enlargement. Other light sources (excepting tungsten lamps) may also show variation of intensity with time of burning—a photometer will clearly show when the light has reached consistent intensity.

Vibration. Vibration must be avoided, especially with vertical enlargers. Impact of the body against the worktable, vibrations caused by machinery or by persons walking close by in the building, or by heavy traffic, may cause loss of definition—especially with enlargements of high magnification.

Reflections. These can be troublesome, and sometimes are hard to locate. The best way to detect a source of reflection is to examine the enlarging camera and its environment by a mirror directed from the plane of the enlarging easel. Harmful reflections can arise from bright metal enlarger supports, overbright walls catching light from the vents of the enlarger, light or polished objects on the worktable that fall within the field of the projected image, the beveled edges of the paper holder, etc. Some of these effects may not be seen when you are standing at the side of the enlarger.

---

* If a photometer is used, the intensity of the enlarging light (on the lens axis at the paper plane and without the negative in place) should be listed along with other data.

PROBLEMS OF CONTROL

It is unfortunate that the average concept of enlarging is based more on technical aspects than on creative image quality. Granted that the elements of scale, definition, grain, and the emotional impact of the image must all be considered, it is my conviction that the spectator should never be influenced to think "If that is a contact print, *this* must be an enlargement!" The photographic statement should be logical and complete, and transcend the mechanics employed.

However, even with perfect equipment and competent procedure the control of print quality in enlarging is sometimes very difficult. With a planned negative —that is, a negative in which the opacity range is designed expressly for enlarging purposes with the particular equipment used—these difficulties are minimized. Yet the problems vary with different degrees of enlargement; enlargement of a given negative to 8x10 will give certain effects not observed in the contact print; enlargement to 16x20 introduces other effects; and so on. These effects are both technical and esthetic; some are discussed in the following paragraphs.

Optical and Technical Considerations

Perspective depends upon the distance from the lens to the subject photographed, regardless of focal length of lens, subject field, or size of negative. A literal impression of the perspective is gained when the image is viewed from a distance similar to the focal length of the lens used in making the negative (see Book 1, p. 23). To be more precise, the actual distance of the lens from the negative—the effective focal length—is the controlling factor, for when working with close subjects the lens is extended beyond its basic focal length. Now if the negative is enlarged 2 times, the viewing distance should be doubled to retain the same perspective effect. This must be carefully considered in making photomurals; the viewing distance may have no proportionate relationship to the lens-to-negative distance in the camera used. Of course I am speaking of a realistic approach. I beg to remind the reader that definite *departure from reality* is often to be desired, and the modification of normal perspective effects is a powerful means of producing "unrealistic" effects.

Another important visual factor is the psychophysical "scanning" of the image. We know that the eye sees clearly only a very small section of the field at any one moment; the construction of the complete impression of the scene is due to the "lingering" of myriad impressions on the retina and brain over a short span of time. The mental and physical effort of scanning a subject is related to the emotional and cerebral response thereto; the more the act of scanning the print matches the act of scanning the original subject, the more "realistic" will the pictorial impression be. Hence there is a considerable difference between an 8x10 image and a 16x20 image—if both are viewed from the same distance. With large photomurals this discrepancy of mood and impact is far more pronounced. Hence the size of the enlargement bears a direct relationship to the emotional effect produced, and we can say that the intensity of the pictorial expression does not depend on sheer size, but on the *appropriate* size for the particular subject.

The problems of grain and definition are discussed in Book 1, pp. 34-35. Textured papers minimize grain, but they also minimize definition and brilliancy of the print image. There is a logical limit to enlargement of the negative where grain and loss of definition (perceived at a given distance) become destructive to the general quality of the image. Also, small black and white areas that may not be objectionable in the contact print may well become very disturbing when enlarged. Hence it is quite conceivable that the proportions of the enlargement (and the selected field) may logically differ from those of the contact print, because of the changes of emotional and formal balance arising from the exaggeration of small forms that may be relatively unimportant in the contact print. Of course, visualization of the final print—whether contact or enlargement—should include awareness of such possible exaggerations of small areas of the image. *Trimming* the print to the visualized composition and proportion is one thing; fortuitously "cropping" of the finished print to find a composition is quite another thing. Yet no hard-and-fast rules should be set down; revisualization of the enlarged image will often reveal hitherto unsuspected qualities and potentialities. This is especially true with enlargements made from miniature-camera negatives, or from negatives made under conditions not permitting careful visualization.

The tonal values of a contact print and an enlargement—even if the same printing light, papers, and developer are used—may differ disturbingly, for several reasons. One is that the disposition of values on a larger area may alter the general effect psychologically although the tone values may be sensitometrically identical. Another reason lies in the reciprocity-departure effect of the paper emulsions. I have been advised that the optimum exposure time for a certain paper should not exceed 30 seconds, for with longer exposures the original exposure scale of the paper is altered. I hesitate to make this a definite statement, for various papers would undoubtedly have different reciprocity-departure characteristics, but the photographer can make tests with the papers he uses and find out for himself what the practical reciprocity-departure effects are for various exposure times. He should first determine the basic exposure for a gray scale, such as the Weston Step Wedge (page 13), with the enlarging lens set at full aperture and focused to about a 1:1 image scale. Then he should double the linear dimensions of the enlargement and give 4 times the exposure; triple the dimensions and give 9 times the exposure, etc. When he has reached the limit of enlargement provided by his equipment, he can then decrease the illumination on the paper further by stopping the lens down, giving double the exposure for each diminishing lens stop. Complete notations should be made on the back of each print, for purposes of comparison and study.

With enlargements of considerable size, do not trust entirely to the eye to ensure perfect focus. Make small tests (working with the more transparent parts of the negative image) simply to check on the sharpness of negative grain or of some small defect such as a pinhole or a small scratch. When perfect focus is achieved (at the lens stop to be used in making the enlargement), tighten both camera and easel adjustments to prevent any change of position during operations.

Do not forget that as exposures are prolonged the possible effect of over-bright room illumination, and reflections from near-by objects that may be in the field of the projected image, will perhaps fog the paper. Also remember that large prints use more developer and fixing bath than do small prints; gauge the volume required generously, according to the amount of print surface to be developed. And, as a final admonition, if the air of the darkroom is of fairly high humidity, the paper may swell and buckle during long exposures—which of course will ruin the image.

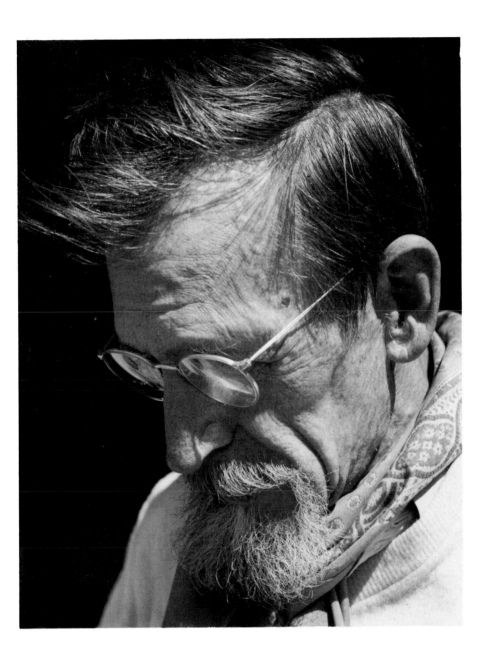

33. Portrait: Maynard Dixon, Tucson, Arizona. This portrait was made against a dark doorway. The negative was exposed to place the skin values (in sunlight) on Zone VII. Normal-minus development was given, and the shadow values (placed on Zone V) have warm middle-gray values in the print. The white sweater is about Zone VII-VIII value, but the right shoulder, catching the sunlight at an acute angle, registers around Zone IX. To augment further the impression of soft, enveloping light, the print was developed in Beers No. 3. A slight selenium tone in the original print enhances the effect of quiet brilliancy.

DETAILED DESCRIPTION OF TONING

There are various aspects of toning, but space permits detailed discussion of only one. The typical example is the direct process of toning in selenium. It is not a difficult process (nor are any of the other standard methods difficult), yet the extremely subtle effect aids in producing a print image of maximum beauty.

In an earlier section on toning (page 24) I expressed my views on print color, and pointed out the difference between an actual color and a subtle modification of blacks and grays. Since it is not possible to reproduce in ordinary letterpress anything that would show the refinements of the toned image in comparison with the untoned image, I urge the photographer to see for himself, through careful experimentation, how great the advantages of toning really are. Here is the step-by-step procedure:

Preparation of the darkroom. Place a bright daylight lamp over the part of the sink to be used for toning. (I use a lamp of 200 watts about 4 feet from the tray.) I advise a daylight lamp for the reason that ordinary tungsten light is too warm; under a warm light I have difficulty in judging the quality of the print color.* Do not leave any other light on in the darkroom during the toning process; the wet print may catch reflections of warmer lights, making it more difficult to judge the tone accurately. I place an untoned print—usually a reject print— in the tray of running water for comparison purposes.

Be certain that the sink is clean. Place a clean tray, preferably of glass or stainless steel (never of chipped enamel, as a trace of rust may cause blue spots on the prints) under the bright daylight lamp, and pour the toner into it. Fill another clean tray with fresh tap water (on or below 68° F) and set it near the toning tray. Into a third clean and rustless tray pour a 2% solution of Kodalk, and place it to the left of the toning tray. Arrange a rinsing tray at the right of the toner, with a light, steady stream of water flowing through it. Prepare the washing sink for immediate use.

Sequence of operation. A print to be toned is first soaked in a tray of water, then placed for 10 to 15 seconds in the Kodalk solution to neutralize any possible residual acidity in the print.** It is rinsed again in the tap water, and then immersed in the toning solution and agitated continuously until toning is completed, when it is rinsed thoroughly, and finally washed and dried. Refer to paragraph 3, page 116.

Take care not to splash toning solution onto the prints soaking in the first tray; it is advisable to keep all untoned prints face down to avoid the possibility of splashing.

---

* The reader may ask why, if the completed prints may be viewed under tungsten light, a tungsten light cannot be used in the process of toning. The chances are that most prints will be viewed in daylight—or combinations of daylight and artificial light—and seldom indeed will viewing illumination be entirely of tungsten quality.

** If you plan to tone a number of prints at once, it is advisable to put them all through the Kodalk bath, then into a tray of water, where they can be kept ready for the next step, the actual toning. When all the prints are so treated, they can be placed in the toning bath (and subjected to constant agitation, of course, if several prints are toned at one time).

It is important that the prints be very thoroughly fixed (preferably in 3 baths—see page 54) and washed before toning. Any remaining trace of silver salts in the emulsion—either from incomplete fixation, fixation in an old bath, or inadequate washing—is likely to produce a general yellowing of the whites. The prints may be still wet from the final washing, or they may have been dried (it is easier to appraise a thoroughly dried print to decide what toning is necessary).

It has been my experience that there is no positive time check on the process of toning; each print seems to require individual judgment. Toning should be controlled entirely by individual preference.

It is safe to assume that with a diluted toner (see formula, page 116) no toning will occur within a minute or so. With a selenium toner, chloride papers tone most rapidly, chlorobromide papers tone slowly, and bromide papers will not tone at all.

Do not keep staring at the print in the toning solution; to do so will make judgment more difficult. Steady watching of the print makes it practically impossible to recognize the growth of the tone. I prefer to look more at the comparison print, glancing occasionally at the print in the toning bath. Suddenly you will become aware that the greenish or bluish-green cast of the untoned print has become neutral. Then (usually) comes a trace of purple tone. At this point, transfer the print from the toning bath to the rinse water. Rinse it a few moments (with agitation), then make a direct comparison with the untoned print. The middle tones will probably show the purplish-brown cast most effectively. The blacks will appear deeper in value (there is actually some intensification of the print). The whites should remain clear. Remember that the print will lose a small amount of its color in washing and drying, so judge the tone accordingly.

If you desire more tone, replace the print in the toning bath—but watch it carefully, for toning may proceed too far for your taste. When the print is toned, put it through the rinsing tray to remove all the solution from the surface, then put it into the washing tank. The print must be in motion during washing; toning continues until the solution in the emulsion is exhausted, and if one print should stick to another in the washing tank, inequalities of tone would probably result.

After the toned prints are thoroughly washed, follow with the subsequent treatments described for prints on page 55. The peroxide-ammonia bath should not be used, but the gold-protective solution (see formula, page 115) will serve to cool the print color slightly, if required. (The G-P solution tends to give a slight bluish cast to either a toned or an untoned print.) I strongly advise against drying with heat—or, for that matter, washing in water warmer than the toning solution. Both seem to lessen the tone, and sometimes remove it entirely. Dry mounting with heat does not seem to harm the dry print, however.

You will observe that the toning may be slightly more noticeable under tungsten light, but shows to best advantage in daylight. The effect is a definite enrichment of values throughout the print; the illusion of luminosity in the print is enhanced.

I have found that a mounting board of the color and quality of Strathmore illustration boards provides a most effective background for prints toned in selenium; the neutral white of the board complements the cool-color value of the prints.

There are a number of toning formulas and some proprietary preparations. I have been satisfied with the Kodak Rapid Selenium Toner, which I use at a dilution of 1 to 10 or 1 to 12. The manufacturer's recommendations include instructions to dilute 1 to 3; this, however, seems suited to adding much more color than I personally prefer. The toning formula on page 116 works exceptionally well. Consult the PHOTO-LAB-INDEX and other texts for descriptions of various toning processes and their effects.

To recapitulate: In selenium toning, follow this procedure:

1. Develop fully.
2. Fix carefully in *at least* 2 baths.
3. Wash thoroughly. Prints may be dried before toning.
4. Immerse in 2% Kodalk solution for 10 or 15 seconds before toning.
5. Rinse and place in a tray of fresh water.
6. Tone with constant agitation (under a bright daylight lamp).

> NOTE: Apparently the higher the dilution, the cooler the tone. Use Kodak Selenium Toner (liquid) at a dilution of 1 to 10 or 1 to 12. Coolness also depends on full development and full fixing and washing.

7. Carry toning a shade beyond the desired point; the print will lose a little tone in washing and drying. Rinse well before placing in the washing sink.
8. Wash the toned print for at least 1 hour.
9. If the tone is a bit too obvious, immerse in the Kodak gold-protective solution (G-P 1). This will "cool" it a bit; it may require about 30 minutes' treatment to be effective.
10. Dry the print without using excessive heat; natural drying is best.
11. Be careful in spotting the print to use a spotting color of matched tone.

Appropriate Mounting Materials for Toned Prints

The average person is prone to think of mounting-board material in terms of white, ivory, brown, etc., and to overlook the extraordinary range of subtle values of color, brightness, and texture available in materials of good quality. Again, he may find it difficult to distinguish between subtle variations of tone under different lighting conditions. Hence comparisons can be made only under light of consistent quality—and comparisons of print color and mount color should also be made under "standard" lighting.

Some types of Bristol board are very bluish in tone; the best-quality boards have considerable brightness; inferior-quality boards are obviously gray in comparison. A fine product, such as Strathmore, will show a marked variation in both color and brightness in the various types of boards available; perhaps the highest brightness is to be had in the plated illustration board. This board also has fine color. It is especially favorable to small prints, giving a mood of preciousness and delicate refinement. Cheap plated boards have a baryta coating, and the basic stock may be very poor underneath.

We can assume that toned prints will never be identical in color or in weight of tone; hence for the most satisfactory effects, the mounting board should be selected for the individual print. I suggest having on hand 15 or 20 samples of mounting board (protected from dirt and abrasion), and making careful comparison with the print under a light of consistent quality and intensity—say a 3200-K lamp at sufficient distance to give a white-card reading of about 20 candles per sq. ft.

34. San Francisco Residence. A subject of high brightness value; brick and wood trim painted a bright cream-white. Values placed one zone higher than normal, and the negative given normal-minus development in Kodak D-23. Print in Kodabromide F No. 2, developed in Beers No. 5 (with 50 cc 1% benzotriazole per liter of working solution). Note the luminosity in the shadows. The steps were slightly printed down to gain a difference of value from the sunlit walls of the building. The convergence was intentional.

35. Wood and Rock, Noon Sun, Sierra Nevada. Normal exposure and development of the negative were possible because of the considerable amount of reflected light directed to the subject from near-by light rocks. The print was made on No. 2 Kodabromide, developed in Beers No. 7 (to intensify the few areas of intense black). In this print, the lower left-hand corner should have been burned down about one zone in visual value. The student should realize that it is seldom possible to achieve the desired print on the first try. A print may be fully prepared for presentation, only to discover some small defect that prompts the photographer to discard the print and start over again. In this particular print, the effect of glaring sun is adequately conveyed, but the composition lacks solidity because of the overbright lower left-hand corner. Note that the values of the print are distributed chiefly in the white, light middle-gray, and black values; a smoother progression of tones might have reduced the impression of glare and harsh brilliancy.

MOUNTING

Mounting of the photographic print is of both physical and esthetic importance. Physically, mounting serves to protect the print and facilitates handling. Esthetically, it serves to present the print to the spectator with maximum emotional impact and with the greatest possible freedom from environmental distractions.

Esthetic considerations must include the proportions of the mount in relation to the proportions—and composition—of the print. The relationship between print color and mount color is also important. There are endless possibilities in adjusting the color and the surface of the mounting board to the qualities of the print, but they need not be discussed here, except to suggest a few practical combinations.

In most cases a fine, smooth-surfaced print requires a smooth, even-toned mount surface of as neutral a white as possible. By "neutral" I mean neither a bluish-white nor a yellowish-white—although certain suggestions of ivory-white relate very well to a print that has been slightly toned in selenium. This ivory or natural-white tone in the mount is an excellent complement to the faint cold-purple sepia tone of the print. The problem is not necessarily to match the color of the print, but to select a mount of harmonizing or complementary value.

Nothing is more distressing to me than the presentation of a smooth-surfaced print on a rough pebbleboard or an off-tone mount.

Black has sometimes been used for photographic overmats. When a black card with a cutout opening is placed over the photograph, the conflict between blacks in the print and the black of the mat can sometimes be very distressing. A similar degree of conflict occurs if the print is mounted on a glaring white card; the whites of the print are degraded, just as the blacks of the print may be degraded by close association with an intense black mat or mount. However, if the black mat is spatially separated from the photograph and the latter is illuminated by a light source between it and the mat, an extraordinary impression of space and depth is obtained. (This would be suitable only for large prints in museums, window display, etc.)

Photographic paper, exposed, developed, thoroughly fixed and washed, and toned to achieve just the right value and color, serves exceptionally well as an overmat or a mount for a print. The surface of this kind of mount can exactly correspond to the surface of the print, yet have a different tonal value. The processed paper must be carefully mounted on firm cardboard for the required rigidity; owing to the excessive tendency of photographic papers to curl, it is advisable to mount a piece of the same paper, emulsion side out, on the reverse side of the card.

For the most satisfactory effects, the proportions of the mount and the position of the print on the mount should relate to the proportions, content, composition, and tonal weight of the print. This implies a mount of different size for almost every photograph. The only arguments against this system relate to problems of storage and display. A compromise lies in establishing a certain size and proportion of mount, and placing the print thereon in a position of maximum balance. One standard museum size is 14¼x19¼, but in recent years size 14x18 has become popular. The next larger standard exhibit size is 16x20. Of course there is no reason why the photographer cannot determine the size—or sizes—

most pleasing to him personally. Edward Weston uses 14x15½ mounts (horizontal), or 13½x16¼ (vertical), which are especially favorable to the proportions of his prints. I use 14x18 mounts for prints approximating 8x10, and 11x14 mounts for 4x5 and 5x7 prints. As mounting board usually comes in 28x36 and 22x28 sizes, 14x18 and 11x14 mounts can be cut from these larger sizes with no waste.

When we have decided on the standard size of our mount, our first consideration is the approximately correct position of the print on the mount. If we think of prints as having dominant either a vertical or a horizontal movement, and so of either vertical or horizontal form, it becomes highly illogical to defeat this dominant movement by using a mount of opposing shape. I believe that mounting a vertical print on a horizontal board, or mounting a horizontal print on a vertical card, almost always destroys the impression of movement and the vitality of the image. In Figure 36 a we note a satisfactory placement of a vertical print on a vertical mount, and in Figure 36 b a satisfactory placement of a horizontal print on a horizontal mount. Figure 36 c shows bad placement of a horizontal print on a vertical mount. Figure 36 d shows a questionable unconventional placement of a print on the mount. (Unconventional placements may have emotional value, though, if the relationships between print composition and organization of the print on the card are well worked out.

A simple rule for mounting on vertical cards (which, however, may often produce rather sterile effects) is to have side and top margins equal, without regard for the lower margin. In my own work, I prefer to have the side margins equal, but I allow considerable flexibility in the relation between top and bottom margins. In fact, if an impression of height and space is desired, the top and bottom margins may be equal, or the top margin may even be greater than the bottom margin.

When the print is trimmed to its final proportions, it should be laid on the mount and moved about until its position appears most pleasing; then two tiny pencil points may be made on the mount to designate two corners of the print. After an interval of time, the position of the print may again be experimented with; if the first position still seems most acceptable, the photographer can feel assured that he has done the best he can in the placement of the print on the mount.

I stress once more that in the presentation of the print to the spectator, the print and the mount should be made into a single expressive unit. Careless and inappropriate mounting can seriously reduce the effectiveness of the finest photograph.

The mounting board should be of firm structure, to prevent curling or damage from repeated handling. It must be composed of durable materials. Many of the ordinary mounting materials are not permanent; the laminations may separate, the color may degenerate, and the board may disintegrate. If the photograph is really worthy of perpetuation, it should be mounted on the finest material obtainable. Such excellent materials as the Strathmore illustration boards—although more expensive than the ordinary boards—are most economical in the long run.

Dry mounting is by all odds the best method of mounting prints. It is clean, dependable, and least likely to damage the print. We will later discuss this process at great length. Other means sometimes used for mounting photographs include:

36. Placement of Prints of Various Proportions on Mounts. See text, page 84, for explanation.

1. *With rubber cement.* Rubber cement should never be used for mounting fine prints. There is not only the danger of eventual permanent stain, but also the difficulty of making the print lie neat and flat on the mount.

2. *With paste or glue.* To do a good mounting job with paste or glue demands experience and great care. With paste, the print and/or the mount should first be dampened. Then the adhesive is evenly applied over the entire back of the print, the excess is wiped off, and the print is carefully placed in position on the mount. The danger lies in the probability of smearing the exposed surface of the mount. Mounting with glue or mucilage is carried out in a similar way, but is potentially even more dangerous to the mount. (Careless application of a few dabs of glue or paste to the back of the print will, without exception, result in curled edges and in pucker marks that will show on the surface of the print.) Following mounting with these adhesives, the prints should be protected with several sheets of soft, absorbent paper and placed under slight pressure to dry.

The mounting of large photomural prints is described on page 106. If paste or glue is to be used, the best and most practical method is to mount the photograph, back to back, on another sheet of similar photographic paper—or on thin cardboard backed with another sheet of photographic paper—then to trim the ensemble to the desired size and proportion and attach it to the mount with a number of small touches of glue on the back of the print. (Be sure to be sparing of the glue, and to apply it far enough back from the edges to prevent any possible oozing out over the surface of the mount when the necessary pressure is applied.)

Dry Mounting

This process requires a dry-mounting press (although a large electric iron suffices for small prints), several sheets of firm smooth cardboard (to place between platen and print and between print and base), and a supply of good mounting tissues. Dry-mounting tissue is a white shellac substance (a thermoplastic) in the form of thin sheets cut to various sizes or obtainable in long rolls. This substance softens under the application of a certain amount of heat and impregnates fibrous materials, such as paper, thereby binding them together in a waterproof unit. Several varieties of tissue are on the market, some with a far lower softening temperature than others, but all are of approximately equal effectiveness.

The method of application is simple. The back of the print is dusted off and a piece of dry mounting tissue is laid over it and "tacked" to the print. (The standard "tacking iron" is simply a small, electrically heated implement, not unlike a soldering iron, with a flat surface about 1 inch square, which is drawn over the tissue and softens it so that it adheres to the print.) We must be sure that the flat part of the iron rests evenly on the tissue; if the edges of the iron are pressed against the tissue, ridges may be formed on the surface of the print. The direction of the motion of the iron should be *outward*, away from the center of the print. If it is toward the center, the tissue may bunch up, causing visible ridges or bumps on the surface of the print after mounting.

Some workers trim the mounting tissue to the exact size of the print (or less by perhaps 1/32 inch) and then attach the tissue to the print. This is an unnecessarily arduous method. I advise attaching a sheet of tissue the same size as or larger than the untrimmed print to the back of the print and then trimming print and tissue together. The tacking iron should be drawn over the tissue as shown in Figure 37 a. For small prints, only the diagonal lines of adhesion are required, but for larger prints right-angle lines will be helpful in holding the tissue securely to the print and thereby avoiding creeping during the trimming. Note that the lines of application do not extend to the extreme corner or the extreme edge. Figure 37 b indicates an error that should be avoided. If the adhesive line runs to the extreme corner or edge, then when the trimmed print is placed on the mount it will prove impossible to lift up a corner or an edge of the print to get the iron under it to tack the print to the mount. Figure 37 c is another example of wrong tacking.

The print may be trimmed roughly to final size before the application of the tissue, then trimmed to accurate size afterward. During the trimming it is well to prevent possible creeping of the tissue by holding the entire edge of the print firmly under a piece of heavy cardboard pressed just within the trim line. After mounting, any excess tissue would show up as a thin glistening line.

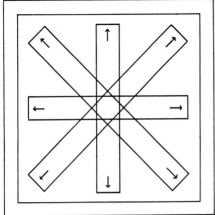

37a

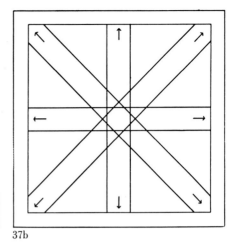

37b

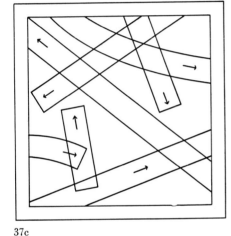

37c

37. Schematic Diagrams of Methods of Attaching (Tacking) Dry-Mounting Tissue to the Backs of Prints:

37a. The proper method; tissue evenly tacked to the print, with provision for lifting corners or edges for tacking to the mount.

37b. This method—tacking print to extreme corners and edges—does not admit lifting of corners or edges to allow tacking to the mount.

37c. A haphazard tacking—may result in difficulty in attaching print to mount, and also may produce visible ridges on the surface of the mounted print.

After the print with the tissue tacked to it is finally trimmed, it is placed in the desired position on the mount and a weight (such as a smooth glass paperweight) is used to hold the print firmly on the mount until the loose edges of tissue are attached to the mount with the tacking iron. Be certain that there are no specks or wrinkles under the print; they might show up as annoying bumps on the surface of the mounted print. With the print held firmly in the proper position, one corner or edge is lifted and the tacking iron is gently inserted between print and tissue, pressing the tissue against the mount with a downward and slightly outward stroke. (If the tacking iron pushes toward the center of the print, it is likely to cause a ridge in the tissue; if it is pulled outward too far, it may soil the mount with the softened substance dragged over it by the tacking iron. In effect, this tacking motion is a sequence of downward, outward, and upward movements.) Then an opposite corner is tacked to the mount in the same way. In working with large prints, two opposite edges should be similarly attached to the mount, to prevent any possible shift of the print while the ensemble is being placed in the mounting press.

When the print is securely attached by corners or edges, it is dusted off and placed in the mounting press and the cover board is inspected to make sure that it has no dust or roughness on its surface; then it is placed over the whole assembly and pressure and heat are applied.

The schematic diagram of Figure 38 shows the various elements in place in the dry-mounting press. First there is the firm bed of the press, and then a felt pad designed to equalize pressure due to the inequalities of thickness of other elements. Then a thin piece of paper is laid over the felt to prevent any possible soiling of the print. (Note that the felt pads may absorb moisture from the heated boards and in time may stain the back of the mounts.) Then come the mounting board, the tissue, and the print, and over that the two thicknesses of cardboard. The surface of the board next to the print should be *very* smooth and soft. The combined thickness of this cover board should be about ⅛ inch. While it will require a slightly longer application of heat and pressure when such thickness of cover board is used, the distribution of heat will be more even, and there will be less chance of buckling due to the sudden application of heat to substances of different expansion properties. If the press at its full operating heat is applied to the mounted print with only a thin cover board, serious curling and buckling may occur, and perhaps damage to the print surface.

Before mounting the prints, the cover board and the mounts should be subjected separately to several minutes of heat with light pressure, and then exposed to air; this process will expel moisture contained in the board. In humid regions the boards take up considerable moisture, and if this is not removed, the print may stick disastrously to the cover board.

The temperature of the dry-mounting press should be around 175° F. If it is too cool, the tissue will merely stick to the print and not to the mount, and if too hot, the tissue will adhere to the mount and not to the print. It must be remembered that too great and too prolonged heat will disintegrate the mounting tissue and destroy its adhesive power.

After mounting, the print should be removed and the mount bent rather severely from the corners. If the adhesion is insufficient, the print will snap away from the mount. The remedy is reapplication of heat and pressure in the press. The mounted print should be allowed to cool on a smooth table under a weight of several pounds; otherwise curling may result. After the print is cooled, it should be tested again by sharp bending; if the adhesion is still perfect, it is safe to assume that the print will not separate from the mount. If the print should separate from the mount, it may always be given another application of heat, but paste or glue or other adhesives should never be used on it.

When flatirons are used, the same procedure obtains throughout except that the iron is moved slowly over the cover board above the print. An equal application of heat must be assured for every part of the print. In this case, the iron can be heated to a very considerable temperature; a little experience will show how much motion is required to transmit the proper amount of heat through the cover board to the print. The cover board must be of adequate thickness (⅛ inch), and the iron must never be allowed to remain in one position, lest an impression of its outline appear on the surface of the print. If the heat is too great, an actual visible change in the surface brilliance of the print may take place. The cover board must never be rubbed across the print during mounting, as it may abrade the surface of the print.

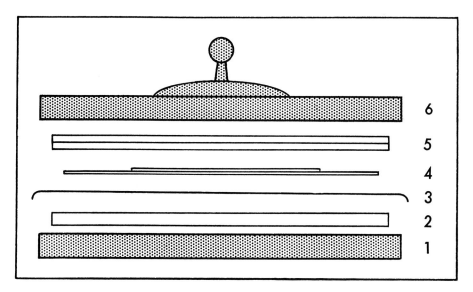

38. Schematic Diagrams: Dry-Mounting Press Assembly. (1) Firm base of press. (2) Felt pad. (3) Sheet of tough paper. (4) Mount with print attached. (5) Sheet of heavy cardboard—or, better, two sheets of medium-weight cardboard—with very smooth side facing print. (6) Platen containing heating elements.

Prints may be mounted in relief by mounting first on a thin cardboard and trimming to the desired proportions and then attaching this ensemble to the mount, either with dry-mounting tissue trimmed to within ⅛ inch of the size of the print or by the application of small dabs of mucilage. The great advantage of mounting prints this way is that if the mount is damaged, it is relatively easy to remove the print and remount it, but if the print is attached directly to the mounting board it is practically impossible to remove it without seriously damaging both.

For mounting prints that are larger than the platen of the mounting press, the cover board should cover the entire mount and the ensemble should be placed under the press with the platen covering one corner of the mount at a time. The action is applied to each corner in rotation until the print is completely secured to the mount. The platen should always generously overlap the area of the previous and the following applications. Any area of the print that does not receive a sufficient application will probably show as a raised area. If the cover board does not cover the entire print, its edge may produce a depression on the surface of the print; furthermore, if the boards are laminated, moisture from within may steam out at the edges of the cover board and leave a mark on the print or the mount.

Failure in dry mounting is most frequently caused by specks and roughness lying between tissue and print or tissue and mount, or on the surface of the cover board next the print. Insufficient or uneven application of heat and pressure will certainly cause trouble.

While the foregoing may sound excessively elementary in character, each step is of the greatest importance. Photography, like the proverbial chain, is as strong as its weakest link. I can think of nothing more distressing than to find a beautiful print ruined by some avoidable defect in the process of mounting.

39. The Watch Tower, Mesa Verde National Park, Colorado. The negative of this picture is quite similar to that of Figure 24 of Book 2. All values are rather exaggerated; both the lighting and the subject values were very flat. Expansion of values was achieved in both the negative and the print. Few true whites or blacks are to be found; the lightest area on the tower is printed to about Zone VIII value; deepest values in the foreground printed to about Zone I value. Total black appears only in the windows in the tower. The vitality of the print was considerably increased by a slight amount of selenium toning.

90

ETCHING AND SPOTTING OF PRINTS

The etching and spotting of prints should not be confused with retouching, coloring, etc. The former are perfective treatments, and do not alter the basic character of the photograph.

Etching

This is a potentially dangerous process. Specks and scratches in the negative that will print dark should be repaired directly on the negative whenever possible. The chemical reduction of dark spots and streaks on the print is the most satisfactory method, leaving no marks on the print surface, but it is a laborious and rather exacting process. If the defect is very small, it usually leaves a light area around the reduced area, which must then be spotted to match the surrounding tone value. The physical removal of dark defects from the print is almost certain to leave a mark on the print surface that will be seen under light at almost any angle. Such marks are especially unpleasant on glossy surfaces. Even on matte-surface prints, if the abrasion is deep, no treatment that I know of will completely conceal it. Kodak Print Lacquer, and the varnish formulas found in various photographic texts—and Paul Strands' formula, page 118—are effective in minimizing etched or abraded spots on print surfaces of all kinds, including glossy ones. But of course the entire surface of the print should be treated to preserve equal reflectance.

The technique of etching requires much practice. The tendency is first to *dig* out the dark defects. The effect is obvious—a crater in the emulsion, even down to the paper base. The proper technique is to use a very sharp blade with a gently rounded point, and to scrape the surface of the defect very lightly, holding the blade perpendicular to the surface of the print. The treatment should be so light that it will require many strokes to wear down the dark spot; progress can be observed by continual examination through a magnifying glass. A dark line can be reduced by short, light scrapings in the direction of the line, not working at any one place too long, but returning again and again to previously worked spots, and judging the allover effect rather than the treatment at any one part of the line. Eye fatigue must be guarded against.

If the scraping has been kept light, resoaking and drying the unmounted print will help reduce the roughening. Occasionally rubbing the area hard with a silk handkerchief will equalize the surface. The application of a glossy lacquer with a small brush sometimes gives gratifying results, especially with deeper abrasions of the surface.

As with spotting, etching of the print should be perfect enough to assure an acceptable effect at normal viewing distance. The more continuous the surrounding tones (such as sky), the more difficult it is to do an invisible job. The best remedy is to clear up as many defects as possible in the negative.

Spotting

This is the correction of light specks and lines produced in the print by opaque defects in the negative, or by dust particles on the negative, printing-frame glasses, etc. Elimination of these defects is vastly simpler than the removal of dark defects. Yet it requires a careful technique and much patience.

·If the print is made on a matte or semimatte surface, practically any type of spotting material—either an opaque substance or a dye—is satisfactory, especially if the print is to be varnished or sprayed afterward. The spotting colors should be blended to match the print color.

If the print is on a smooth, glossy surface (such as an unferrotyped glossy paper) the problem is not so simple. A spotting material may have a lower reflective index than the paper surface, and will appear as a disturbing dull spot. It is then better to use opaque materials of high reflective value, or to resort to the use of dyes. (For purposes of reproduction—such as lithography or halftone —a difference of surface shine causes little trouble.)

I use double-weight glossy papers, unferrotyped, for most of my prints, and with them I avoid surface effects by using these methods of spotting:

1. Dye spotting. Dyes such as Spot-Tone have the advantage of darkening an area without appreciably affecting the surface reflectance. Dye spotting is most advantageous when no really heavy blacks are required. A disadvantage of dye spotting is that not all dyes are stable; some have a tendency to turn blue. Applications of a dye may be partially or entirely removed by using a dye remover— one recommended for the particular type of dye used.

2. Spotting with pigment of high reflectance. Materials of this type are not easy to obtain in this country. Alfred Stieglitz recommended the following: Schmincke Gloss Retouch Color—Blackish. (M. Grumbacher, New York). I understand this is available. It is somewhat more glossy than the usual spotting colors.

3. Spotting with ordinary India ink in a saturated sugar solution. I have been agreeably surprised at the high reflectivity of this combination, but I seriously caution against the possibility of ants being attracted to prints that have been spotted with a sugar solution. I have had it happen; ants visited an exhibition of prints spotted with this preparation and crowded between the mounts and cover glass seeking the sugar. The damage was considerable.

4. Spotting with ordinary India ink mixed with gum arabic. Refer to formula on page 118 (kindly given me by Edward Weston). This gives an application of rich black (other values as properly diluted and applied) with a fine brilliant gloss that closely matches the surface of an unferrotyped glossy print.

No matter what the material used, the application of the spotting colors to the print requires care and patience. First, a *good* brush is essential. I use a No. 0—sometimes a No. 00—but often a larger brush will have a fine taper and a "workable" tip, both essential to efficient spotting. A brush may be expensive and carry a fine name but may be hopeless for spotting prints. Only trial and error will serve to select a really satisfactory brush for this purpose. When spotting is to be undertaken, the worktable must be clean, equipment and materials placed at hand, and the print adequately illuminated with light of slightly more than normal viewing intensity. The surface is first cleaned off, to remove all dust that might look like actual spots. The spotting colors are mixed to match the general value and color of the print; they are tested by applying to a sheet of plain photographic paper. Let us consider first the problem of spotting a sky of middle-gray value. Suppose there are a number of small specks and a faint line (suggesting a scratch in the negative). We first blend the spotting material to the proper value and color and test it on a white paper. Then we apply a small amount of color—with a fine, well-pointed brush—to one of the spots. If it is too heavy, we can remove it or reduce it immediately with a slightly damp cloth (applying light pressure). We can observe from this how well we have matched the spotting material. We may find that we get more even effects with a drier brush; that is, a brush from which the larger part of the spotting solution has been removed by wiping it on a piece of plain paper before touching it to the print. Several applications with a "dry" brush will usually give better results than one application with a wet brush. The surface coating on the paper affects the "taking" of the spotting material. Addition of a small amount of wetting agent to the spotting material sometimes helps. If skin oil from contact with hands or fingers makes it difficult to apply the spotting material, the print should be wiped carefully with a clean linen cloth; in bad cases it may be treated with a mild solvent.

The spotting should be adequate to render defects unnoticeable at normal viewing distance. It is better to underspot slightly than to overspot. If an area is almost but not quite dark enough, it may be best to bring it to the desired tone by lightly touching the area with a medium pencil and then rubbing it gently with a soft cloth.

Where a white spot must be corrected in a heavy black area, it is obvious that the spotting material must be applied in rather concentrated form. It is better to give several applications of moderately deep spotting color than one application that may prove too heavy or spread over the adjacent print surface. In an area of heavy continuous tone even dye spotting will probably show as a slightly dull surface.

Where a very faint speck or line must be removed I have often found it satisfactory to rub the print first lightly with a soft cloth (thereby removing traces of oil from fingers, etc.) and then to apply lightly a medium pencil, again rubbing the print lightly afterward, and again applying the pencil if necessary. Never press hard; that is certain to leave a permanent mark. Although I say here a medium pencil, actually the surface hardness of the print dictates what grade of pencil will take best. And paper-surface hardness in turn depends somewhat on the processing given it as well as on its inherent qualities.

Always protect the surfaces of both print and mount when spotting. A large sheet of paper with a small opening in it, which can be slid over all parts of the print, is excellent protection. The paper should be *black*, to minimize glare and eyestrain, and to make the spotting more efficient. There is nothing more exasperating than to drop the spotting brush on the mount, or otherwise accidentally blemish the print or the mount during spotting. Also, resting the hand on the print or the mount may leave visible marks; at least it will transmit some skin oil to the surface.

When the areas to be spotted—that is, lowered in tone—are large, real skill is required. It requires extraordinary technique to give the entire area a continuous tone of the proper value and color. An easier and more practical way is to stipple the areas, so that defects such as inequalities in sky value (due to inadequate agitation in development or to defective emulsion) may be equalized. Also, these areas can often be corrected by careful airbrushing and subsequent varnishing or spraying with lacquer. I choose to take my print to an expert airbrush operator when such drastic treatments are required.

Always remember that when a print is varnished or sprayed with a transparent lacquer or plastic, the spotting colors usually deepen in tone, and allowance should be made for this in judging the degree of spotting required.

I emphasize a basic principle in my approach to photography: Spotting is a justifiable corrective procedure, applied to augment the perfection of the photographic statement, and should be distinguished from *retouching*, which involves the alteration of line, texture, or value without regard for the integrity of the straight photographic process.

Surfacing of Prints

If prints are on a glossy unferrotyped paper, surfacing is seldom necessary. However, if prints have had much etching and spotting, or have been scratched or otherwise damaged, some surfacing may be required.

After etching and spotting, prints that are made on matte or semigloss surfaces may be treated with any of a variety of substances designed to give luster and high reflectance, applied by brush or spray. These materials must meet these requirements: 1) They must have high transparency; 2) they must be colorless—and remain so indefinitely; 3) they must be free of impurities or lumps; 4) they must impart augmented brilliance to the print.

Applying wax, varnish, lacquer, or plastics by dipping, brush, or cloth always invites the possibility of streaks and uneven areas. To my mind the only way to treat the surface of a print properly is to spray the substance over it with a rather powerful airbrush. The spread of the cloud of mist should be large enough to prevent bands of unequal application that would show when the print is dry. I have found that after the first allover application of a lacquer or plastic I can do further refined spotting, and then apply subsequent coats.

A waterproof surface has the advantage of being cleanable with a damp cloth —a definite advantage in photomurals, photo screens, and overmantels, where no glass protects the print.

Photographs may be laminated between two sheets of transparent plastic, but if the process requires excessive heat the print will probably change color. For special effects for decorative purposes, certain subtle colors can be added to the surfacing materials. But if this cannot be done to perfection, it had best not be attempted at all.

I do not recommend mounting varnished prints with the dry-mounting press. It is better to mount the print first on a light card, trim both print and card together as desired, treat with the surfacing material, and then attach the print-card ensemble to the large mount by glue or mucilage.

The protection and the presentation of prints are discussed on pp. 91-96 of Book 1. These subjects merit careful study. Remember that a fine photographic print is a rather delicate thing, quite vulnerable to scratching and soiling. Apart from the physical value of the print, the psychological effect of cleanness and perfection, and of appropriate presentation, cannot be minimized. A trim portfolio in which prints are kept with good interleaves (I suggest a Strathmore drawing surface, 1-ply, as this material is far more enduring than ordinary tissue paper) is essential for fine prints. Albums with leaves of fine white mounting board, with interleaves to protect the prints if they are mounted face to face, and bound in firm covers and plastic rib binding are always attractive. Prints may be set in plastic folds for protection but such covering material—no matter how clear— will slightly reduce the brilliancy of the print.

MAKING PRINTS FOR REPRODUCTION

This is a subject which deserves more attention than it has been given. In fact, the general *practical* knowledge relating to most phases of the problem is scant and contradictory. I have been attempting for years to find some simple rationale, but without avail. The majority of engravers and lithographers appear to work on an empirical approach, so far as determination or description of the values of the original subject is concerned. As a photographer I know that the various processes—halftone, lithography, gravure, collotype, etc.—are capable of reproduction of certain scales of brilliancy (or, more technically, reflection density). Much depends on the reflectivity, the color, and the surface of the photographic printing papers, but let us work on the assumption that papers and ink of maximum brilliance are to be used by the printer, so that the maximum scale of the process itself is realized. Now, what type of print should be made to best "fit" offset litho, halftone, collotype, photogravure, rotogravure, etc.? If the intention is to *reproduce* the qualities of the original print, how must the "copy"

40. Gas Station, Chemurgic Company Plant, Richmond, California. (E. T. Spencer, architect.) Nowhere in this subject will be found pure whites; the highest values are those of sunlit concrete. Normally these values would be on Zone VII; here, to preserve the impression of luminosity and sunlight, they are rendered as Zone VIII. The lowest values approximate Zone I. In the original print, the textures of the concrete are clearly revealed.

print* be adjusted in tonal scale so that the reproduced printing-press image will most satisfactorily realize this intention?

I cannot give any specific information on the desired brilliancy (reflection density) scale of prints for any particular reproduction process. I have asked the question as to this numberless times, and rarely receive similar answers. A moment's thought will convince the reader that knowing the total brilliancy range of the print is not enough; the shape of the brilliancy (reflection-density) curve is of great importance. We all recognize the fact that the blacks of offset lithography are relatively weak compared to those of halftone. Hence with offset lithography a greater separation of values in the deeper parts of the copy print is desirable. We are all conscious of the frequent "blocking" of the light values in halftone reproductions. Obviously, exaggeration of separation of the lighter values is necessary for good halftone reproduction. Collotype has a range of about 1 to 25 (reflection density of 1.4). It gives maximum detail, but I have found that both deep and light values are relatively weak. I am speaking here, of course, of the reproduction of an original sharp glossy print of maximum brilliance; a soft "pictorial" print may be better reproduced with gravure, collotype, or offset litho than with halftone. The early platinum prints of Stieglitz were magnificently reproduced in photogravure; the relatively harsh full-scale impact of the modern halftone would not have been entirely appropriate. (Excepting the magnificent reproductions by the Lakeside Press, Chicago, for the *Stieglitz Memorial Portfolio*, Twice-a-Year Press, New York, N. Y.).

Generally speaking, separation of print values is of equal importance to total brilliancy scale. Tones that are too close in value may be disappointingly blended in reproduction. In making pictures for ordinary newspaper reproduction, we should attempt to compose the image so that values in juxtaposition are of maximum difference. It has been said that a good newspaper halftone will adequately reproduce 5 steps of tone—black, white, and 3 steps of gray. For most definite effects, similar values should not be allowed to merge—white or light gray should be placed against black, black or dark gray against white, etc. The best newspaper photographers have this "engraver's sense" and visualize images in broad simple compositions with strong tonal separations.

When asked what kind of print they most desire, engravers will usually say, "Give me a snappy print" or "I like a contrasty print."

To judge a print for reproduction merely by "contrast" or "snap" is a dangerous concept, and leads to all kinds of miserable results. However, engravers have admitted that there is no definite standard; the personal variations among engraving technicians are numerous—what may be good copy for one engraver may give another great trouble.

This is a very unfortunate situation, and it is a mystery to me why it has not been cleared up by now. After all, photoengraving is a photographic process; the engraver's negative has a definite exposure scale and contrast range. The reflection density of the printed reproduction can be measured; it depends on the quality of the engraving, the quality and application of the ink, and the reflective values of the paper. A reproduction on the printed page can be evaluated in terms of reflection density just as a photographic print can.

---

* I use the term "copy" here in the publishing sense—original manuscript, photographs, etc. to be reproduced are known collectively as "copy." Do not confuse this meaning with "copy" in reference to a *photographic copy of an original print*, drawing, or document.

96

In general, for reproduction purposes I print rather "soft" and deep. I retain detail in the deepest shadow values, and always try for some area of maximum black. I print my pure whites (Zone IX values and above) as pure white—but I print my textured whites (Zone VIII) down to about Zone VII value. The copy print looks very dull and heavy, but an intelligent and sympathetic engraver finds that all the values are well within the limitations of his own process. He may then expand the contrast range to the limit of his process: Zone IX values appear pure white, Zone VIII values appear as high textural whites, not blocked out. The deep values are also retained, and the reproduction approaches the full tonal scale of the "fine print."

An experience of my own is illustrative: In 1938 the Lakeside Press made a series of remarkable reproductions of my photographs for a special publication —*Sierra Nevada, The John Muir Trail.* Many of the reproductions have astonishing fidelity to the original fine print in both tonal scale and surface brilliance. (They were made with a 175-line halftone screen, and the finest type of glossy paper, subsequently coated with a plastic surfacing.) For reproduction, in practically every case it was necessary for me to make a print in which the lightest values were intentionally depressed, as the brilliancy scale of the original fine print exceeded the capacity of the engraver's materials. By reducing the total brilliancy scale of the print—and thereby exaggerating textural effects in the lightest values of the image—I provided the engraver with a compacted but *complete* scale favoring tonal separations in the highest values. With these, the engraver was able to record all the values on his plate, and it was his problem to increase the contrast of his image to the point where maximum possible scale was achieved in the printing press. Of course this manipulation requires good taste on the part of the engraver, the finest obtainable paper and printing craftsmanship, and a fine print on which the engraver can base his standards of comparison.

Do not be misled by claims that a halftone of very fine screen always gives better-quality images. I have found by experience that a screen of 150 lines per inch gives the best effect on ordinary good coated paper stock. On fine stock a screen of 175 can be used. Finer screens, while giving more detail and resolution of image, have a tendency to block in the deeper values unless printed by a master pressman on the finest obtainable paper.

Some Factors Influencing Quality of Reproductions

1. Proper scaling of values of the print for the reproduction process used
2. Proper surface of the print (glossy or smooth surfaces preferred)
3. Proper color of the print (blue-black usually preferred)
4. Technical ability of the engraver
5. Taste and sensitivity of the engraver as to subtle photographic qualities
6. Taste and sensitivity, and technical ability, of the printer
7. Paper of adequate surface and color
8. Ink of appropriate value and color and reflectance
9. Subsequent surfacing of reproductions by varnishing or lacquering
10. Mutual understanding between photographer, engraver, and printer on what the final result shall be. If the reproduction relates to a professional assignment, the client should certainly be brought into the discussions. Many failures in quality are due to lack of common understanding by all parties.

41. The White Church, Hornitos, California. (From *Portfolio One*, by Ansel Adams, 1948.) This is a reproduction of a "mass-production print" of the most exacting quality. The reproduction cannot convey the subtlety of the textures in the white church, nor the richness of the black fence shadows. The consistent quality of the prints (about 100 were made) derived from careful exposure control and equally careful development of the prints. The print was made in a "aero" printer, containing 9 lamps and 2 sheets of ground glass. It required about a day to set up the printer and arrange the necessary dodging elements on the ground-glass sheets and cut off a few of the lights. Relatively little dodging or burning was required; the central shadow was slightly lightened, and all-round edge burning was added (about 5% of the total exposure). There was no local burning of the white church; the delicate textures of the church were barely perceptible in the wet print; in the dry print they appeared just right. But to determine this, test prints were made and thoroughly dried before establishing the correct exposure and developing procedures.

MASS PRODUCTION OF PRINTS

I refer here to moderate production in the photographer's laboratory, not to the machine-controlled mass production in commercial plants. I am assuming that the photographer is concerned with work of the highest quality, and I desire to present a method whereby, with simple equipment, he can make one hundred or more fine prints a day. I have been distressed by the frequent overemphasis on the single "fine" print—the one and only print—and by the average photographer's dread of undertaking production of a quantity of fine prints.

It is my conviction that if the desired result is clearly visualized, and if an adequate mechanical procedure is established, any number of perfectly consistent prints can be made to match the first "pilot" print. With a good procedure, matching is relatively simple; frequently I have given more time to getting this pilot print than to the making of a hundred subsequent prints. Consistency is the chief mechanical objective. This depends upon:

1. Using the same brand, type, and run of paper

2. Using printing or enlarging lights of consistent intensity (with provision for voltage control if the line current fluctuates)

3. Using the same developer formula throughout (with the same dilution, temperature, and content of restrainer)

4. Using the same ample quantity of developer for each equal batch of prints, and agitating the prints constantly during development

5. Giving prints equal fixation, washing, toning, and final washing, and submitting them to similar drying conditions

Obviously, the production of many prints at one time implies ample darkroom and finishing-room space. Possibly the most serious bottleneck is the print-drying area. One hundred 8x10 prints require at least 10,000 square inches of surface, or at least seven 2x5 feet cheesecloth racks. (Remember there must always be a small space between the prints lying on the racks.) Another bottleneck is in the darkroom: adequate wet storage for prints after the first fixation. (This is discussed in Book 1, and in this book on pages 61 and 100 the need for the storage tray is described.) On numerous occasions I have produced 200 good prints a day in a relatively small darkroom. I had adequate drying space, but was obliged to wash prints in three batches of about 70 prints each; this operation required over 6 hours. With a larger sink I have processed 250 double-weight prints at one time (washing for at least 2 hours with constant separation and movement of the prints, and emptying the washing sink every 30 minutes). In cool climates where the tap water is 65° F or less, I see no harm in allowing prints to soak overnight and completing the washing on the second day.

Preparation

1. Prepare adequate stock solutions of developer, fixing bath, etc.

2. Be certain you have an adequate amount of paper of the same batch or run (check this by the emulsion numbers printed on the packages). Count and separate batches of 15 or 20 sheets, reserving a few sheets for tests and trial prints.

3. Check on printing and enlarging lights, safelights, and other equipment, including the timer. The timer *must* be accurate and consistent.

4. Prepare developer (see below), stop bath, and first fixing bath. Set up a large storage tray with a constant stream of tap water running through it.

Procedure

1. Make tests as outlined on pages 61 and 62 (remembering to agitate test and trial prints in the developer constantly) until a print of the desired quality is obtained. Thereupon record all essential data, which are to be followed precisely in the exposure and development of every print.

2. Then expose a batch of 15 or 20 prints, and develop them (with constant agitation).

3. When development is complete, place the prints in the stop bath, and agitate them constantly for at least 2 minutes to assure complete neutralization of the developer.

4. As quickly as careful handling permits, place the prints in the first fixing bath. Agitate them constantly for 3 minutes.

5. Place them in the storage tray, giving them ample agitation at first to remove most of the fixing-bath solution, and occasionally checking to see that the running water is adequate to keep them in slight motion. If there is ample space, rinse the prints well before placing them in the storage tray. (If the prints are merely placed in a tray of stagnant water, the action of the fixing bath will continue unevenly. See page 54 for a discussion of optimum fixing time.)

6. Proceed as above with subsequent batches of prints, each with a fresh volumn of developer, until all prints are made. It is advisable to check each batch as a whole against the first pilot print for quality and depth of tone. Also, carefully check the last print of each batch for any obvious physical defect—such as a dust speck on the negative—that would persist in prints of the following batch.

7. When all prints are made, discard developer, bath, and first fixing bath, and clean up the sink. Prepare 2 fixing baths: one of regular type (Kodak F-5 or F-6), which we will call fixing bath 2, and another of plain hypo, which we will call fixing bath 3.

8. Take a batch of 15 or 20 prints from the storage tray and immerse in fixing bath 2. Agitate them for 2 minutes, and then place them in fixing bath 3 and agitate them for 2 minutes.

9. Remove the prints to the washing sink and rinse them in running water with tap flow sufficient to move and separate the prints adequately.

10. Proceed with the remaining batches of prints as above. When all prints are in the washing tank and have been thoroughly rinsed, drain off the water and refill. After 5 or 10 minutes, drain and refill again. Do this about 3 times before the final washing starts; it will remove most of the fixing solution from the prints.

11. Wash for at least 2 hours—3 hours is better—draining off the wash water about every half hour. It is essential that all prints be kept in motion and separated during the entire washing period. To be certain of proper separation, I prefer to take the prints out one by one and place them on the drainboard while the washing tank is emptying. Then, as the tank refills, I replace the prints separately in the wash water. In this way there is little chance for any two prints to stick together for more than a small part of the washing period.

12. When washing is complete, drain, swab, rinse the prints, and set them out to dry. I usually carry this out by placing an entire batch of prints on a drainboard face up. I swab the top print while rinsing it with a light stream of water, then place it face down on another drainboard and swab the back. The next print can be stacked on top of it until all are swabbed front and back. (The clean back of a tray makes a good drainboard. The inside of a tray may be used if it is thoroughly clean, and large enough.)

13. When sufficiently drained, the prints may be laid out face down on clean cheesecloth trays or screens. All water spots should be swabbed off the backs. As an added precaution, I frequently lay the prints on the screens face up and wipe off the excess water with a *clean* viscose sponge before I turn them over, sponge the backs, and leave them to dry.

14. Drying of a quantity of prints will obviously take longer than drying a few prints in the same space. To get ample ventilation I pull alternate screens out as far as they will go; then the prints dry faster than they would if all the screens were close together in the frame. Of course the use of moderately heated air and fans expedites the drying process. However, when the outer prints are dry, I remove them, slide in the empty screens, and pull out the other screens.

15. When sufficiently dry, the prints should be carefully stacked (making sure no dust or grit is between them) and submitted to light pressure, to flatten them.

16. After washing—and before or after drying—the prints may be toned as described on page 78. Here, too, consistency of quality is essential, and the toning should be carried out in a fairly dilute bath so as to give ample time to observe and control the effects. The toning solution should be diluted so as to require at least 4 or 5 minutes, and I do not advise toning more than 12 prints at a time. Use a fresh toning bath for each batch. After toning, the prints are placed in a storage tray and washed again as described above.

17. Trimming, mounting, and spotting a quantity of prints will also require some "production-line" planning. I attach the dry-mounting tissue to the prints (as described on page 86). I then trim them to correspond to the pilot print, and store the prepared and trimmed prints under slight pressure. However, if there is any change of humidity between the time of trimming and the time of mounting, serious trouble may result; if the print expands, the tissue may pull off in spots or cause a warp in the print. If the print contracts, the tissue may buckle, leaving ridge marks that can be seen on the surface of the print after mounting, or it may extrude beyond the margin of the print, showing as a thin glistening line after mounting. If there is any probability of change in humidity, there should be little delay between trimming and mounting.

18. I usually prepare a completed print, and note down the size of the mount and the margin spaces. A cardboard guide can be prepared and used as follows: Attach a right-angled frame of wood to the worktable.* Cut a piece of thick card-

---

* Two rows of small nails in a drawing board can serve equally well as a right-angle guide.

42. Portrait: Priest at Mariposa, California. A subject of high brilliancy; the white vestment against the slightly less white door, and the relatively light skin values (Zones VIII, VII, VI), required careful printing and delicate toning in selenium for maximum effect.

board the width of the right (or left) margin. Mark on this cardboard a line indicating the proper width of the top margin. To use, press the mount into the corner of the frame; press the guide into the same corner over the mount; lay the trimmed print flush against the guide with its top corner at the top-margin line of the guide; place a smooth weight on the print to hold it in place, and "tack" the print to the mount (see page 87). Remove the guide and place the print in a dry-mounting press. If the prints are prepared with the dry-mounting tissue and properly trimmed beforehand, it will be possible to place and "tack" a print on the mount while the preceding print is being mounted in the press. The total time required for mounting 100 prints will approximate 2 hours' steady work (not including attaching tissue to prints and trimming).

Recommended Solutions

1. *Developer.* To develop a quantity of prints one—or a few—at a time would be unnecessarily time-consuming. I use a slow-acting developer, and develop batches of prints for 6 minutes. I find the ideal developer for this purpose is the Ansco 130 formula (Metol-hydroquinone-glycin; formula on page 114). I vary this by omitting the hydroquinone and the potassium bromide, and then when I prepare it for use I mix equal volumes of stock solution and water, and add 25 to 50 cc of 1% benzotriazole per liter of working solution. Any good antifoggant can be used, the proper amount being determined by the fog test (page 61) and by the tone required in the image. For each batch of 20 prints 8x10 I use 2 liters of stock solution diluted with 2 liters of water at 68° F, and then discard it. If softer results are required, I dilute the stock solution further, by 1:2 or 1:3, but I do not increase the amount of the antifoggant. For more contrasty results I use the stock solution without dilution. For still more contrasty results I add one or more 100-cc lots of a straight hydroquinone-sulfite solution (formula on page 114). However, I consider the 1:1 dilution normal, and make my first tests with that. I place the batch of prints—one by one—in the developer as rapidly as possible, and agitate constantly, rotating the pile from bottom to top (under a weak light) for about 6 minutes. Normal development will be practically complete in 4 minutes; there will be practically no change during the extra 2 minutes, but the additional time makes up for the delay in getting the last of the prints into the developer. I recommend making a fog test—both for developer fog and for safelight fog—for 8 to 10 minutes in this developer.

2. *Stop bath.* A 2-liter solution (formula on page 115) is adequate for 20 prints 8x10. I discard it after each batch. (It is poor economy to overwork any photographic solution.)

3. *Fixing bath.* I use the standard fixing baths (F-5 or F-6; formulas on page 115) for the first and second bath, and a plain hypo bath (formula on page 115) for the third bath. I use 3 liters of the first bath for every 50 or 60 prints 8x10, and 3 liters each of the second and third baths for every 100 prints 8x10. If the trays are large enough, I advise using 4-liter quantities. (See page 54 for discussion of fixing baths.)

4. *Toning.* With selenium toning (as described on page 78) I use 1-liter quantities of the Kodalk alkalizing bath and of a toning bath that I prepare by diluting Kodak selenium toner 1:10 or more with water, or whatever dilution is found to produce the desired slight tone in 5 to 6 minutes or more. (Or the selenium toner, formula on page 116, can be used as given or in the required dilution.) I do not put more than 12 prints in 1 liter of the toner at once, and I discard the solution after each batch has been processed.

PHOTOMURALS, OVERMANTELS, PHOTO SCREENS

The term "mural" means "of or pertaining to a wall, or on a wall . . . as a mural painting" (Webster). Esthetically, a mural is a design in any one of various media that is not only *on* the wall, but which is appropriate to it in terms of form, scale, color, design, and function. Hence merely "blowing up" a photographic image and putting it on a wall seldom achieves the best qualities of true mural art. The mechanical and esthetic qualities that must be considered in a photomural include the following:

1. *Image quality.* Because of technical problems, such as the reciprocity departure of the enlarging paper (page 42), image grain, the Callier effect with certain types of enlargers (page 42), and the sheer difficulties of processing, the photographic quality of most big enlargements is poor. Definition is erratic and tonal values are weak. The effects of misalignment of the enlarging camera and easel are particularly evident. The larger the image, the more exacting the technical requirements.

2. *Surface.* For practical purposes the paper used should have a semigloss surface without obvious texture. The larger the image and the greater the viewing distance, the more texture can be tolerated. The illusion of definition may sometimes be augmented by using a fine-textured surface, such as the "silk" surfaces, or the E, G, and Y surfaces of Kodak papers. Glossy surfaces are difficult to process in large sizes because they are more subject to breaks and abrasions. When the mural is mounted and spotted, it may be sprayed with a colorless transparent plastic; this increases brilliance, serves to protect the surface, and permits the mural to be safely cleaned. Careful study of the placement of the mural in relation to room lighting is necessary. Its position with respect to windows or lighting fixtures may permit troublesome reflections from the sheen of its surface. In such cases, the mural should be on a matte surface, or shielded from the direct light. If special illumination is provided, it is essential that the illumination be even, and the source far enough away to cover the image completely and avoid uneven brightness in any part. (For example, if the light source is 6 feet from the top of the mural and 10 feet from the base, the brightness ratio will be 36:100, or about 1:3.)

3. *Print color.* This is an extremely important factor; the tone of the print must relate in some way to the general décor of the environment. It may relate directly to the color of the room, or to the complementary color. There is no fixed rule. I am not implying, of course, that there should be an exact match of color; it is usually sufficient to make the print "warm" or "cold" if the general tone of the room suggests either quality. Direct steps toward good color relationship include proper framing, or applying a special background color as a suitable transition from print to general environment. Large prints may be toned in the usual manner, or the surface coating may be slightly colored to give the desired effect.

4. *Print values.* The desired contrast range is, of course, a strictly personal problem. As a rule, a large photomural print should be of somewhat softer quality than a small print of the same subject. A full-tone brilliant mural may be far too dominating, especially in a location where it is frequently seen.

5. *Scale and content.* Again a personal problem. Suffice it to say that the following points are worthy of consideration in planning any mural or overmantel photograph:

a. The subject should be one that does not dominate the thought of the spectator, or limit his fantasy. The usual subjects—landscapes, city views, seascapes, etc.—may be very attractive as *subjects,* but we must remember that a mural installation is a *permanent* installation. What effect will such subjects have on the spectator who lives in close association with the mural? Fatigue and eventual dislike may be induced by a mural the subject of which is literal and regional. It is my conviction that semiabstract subject matter—patterns of leaves, natural or mechanical forms, etc.— wears much better than the usual representative subject matter.

b. Again, we must think of the function of the mural or overmantel: Is it to be installed in a home, where it will be seen under conditions of relaxation; or in an office, where it will dominate the working hours of the occupant; or in a hallway or foyer, where it will be seen only in passing? In each case the problem demands specific treatment. A vigorous design in bold tonalities is acceptable where the spectators are in circulation; in a quiet home or office it might be extremely distracting.

c. The size of the mural or the overmantel as a whole depends, of course, upon available space and the general size of the room. The scale and the content of the mural depend largely on its inherent and environmental mood and on the viewing distance. In a small room, where the viewing distance will usually be about 10 to 16 feet, the mural can be of somewhat complex design and pattern; small and subtle areas of tone and texture can be used to good advantage. But in some large space, such as a foyer or a store, the subtleties may be lost, and the indications should be for bold, simple forms, and definite contrasts of tone.

6. *Presentation.* Simply mounting the mural flat on the wall is probably the weakest presentation. A photograph usually implies *space and depth,* and this effect needs some physical augmentation in the mounting and the presentation of the mural. Murals need not be of large size to give the effect of size; in fact, even a relatively small panel properly placed against the right background can suggest great size and power. I always prefer to have my murals or overmantels mounted on a firm panel, preferably ½-inch plywood, edged with a very thin metal angle rod (aluminum preferred); a ¼-inch overlap on the print edge is all that is required. This whole panel can then be placed about 2 to 4 inches away from the wall (the separation being achieved by hidden supports). In this way a great feeling of depth is achieved. The proper distance from the wall is determined, of course, by a number of complex considerations.

In the case of multiple-print murals (two or more continuous sheets of paper), we can strive to make an exact match (which is never perfect) or we can combine a series of panels, each individually mounted and "edged." Strangely enough, dividing the entire image into sections does not break down the illusion of continuity; rather, it augments the impression of depth. The dividing strips are accepted by the viewer as a screen in space *before* the image. Let us consider a four-panel mural with ¼-inch framing strips; if the panels are 38 inches wide, and the strips ¼-inch, the width of the combined strips with two juxtaposing panels will be only ½-inch, or about 1/75 the width of the single panel. At a distance of 10 feet this is hardly noticeable. In addition, the strips can be toned to approximate the general tonal average of the image. If desired, connecting strips between panels can be T-bars; a crossbar only ¼-inch wide will work perfectly well if the panels are cut accurately and the paper comes neatly to the edge of the panel.

It is possible to mount the print with the edges curled over the sides of the panel; this is effective, but the edges are easily damaged and I do not advise it.

7. *Mounting and trimming.* Mounting technique is of great importance. My advice would be always to have an expert do it! A good picture-framer can usually manage the entire job of mounting and presentation. But take no chances with poor workmanship.

The print *must* be mounted flat—without blisters or ridges, or the surface texture of the board showing through. The panel should be sanded down to a fine smoothness. The print is usually dampened and the adhesive is applied evenly, with especial care that no lumps or hard specks are in it. After the print is applied to the panel, it must be rubbed smooth. This requires great care. The print emulsion is easily damaged when wet (an acid hardener fixing bath must be used in fixing mural prints). When the print is sufficiently smoothed out, the surface must be gone over several times with a soft cloth moderately dampened with clean water, to remove any possible remains of adhesive. When thoroughly dry, the panels are marked for trim, spotted, and sprayed.

If panels with strips between are to be mounted as a continuous whole, it is essential to trim and space the edges of each panel so that proper alignment of individual elements is maintained in the finished mural. Continuous diagonal lines must not "jump" from one panel to another. In trimming, allowance must be made for the thickness of strips or edgings lying between adjacent panels (note that it is only what lies *between,* not *over,* the panel edges that must be considered). Thus if an edging strip is ⅛-inch thick, the panel must be trimmed ⅛-inch *inside* the exact matching line. (If T-shaped strips are used between panels, the allowance on each panel is ½ the thickness of the stem of the T.)

Photo Screens

A photo screen is subject to the same general considerations as a photomural, except that each panel should have a satisfying completeness in itself, since the screen may be folded or placed so that only one or two panels can be seen. The mounting problems are the same, and the panels must be firm, and edged with sturdy metal strips. (Hardwood may be used with discretion.) The hinges should be piano hinges, continuously applied to the inner edges of the panels, and permitting the panels to be folded either in or out from the plane of the fully extended screen. Naturally, the panels must be firm enough and thick enough to take adequate screws through the hinges. The panels may be backed with veneer or fabric.

In a screen, the panels are separated not only by the thickness of the metal stripping, but also by the thickness of the hinges (unless the hinges are countersunk). In any case, the panels should be marked with the exact matching line and then trimmed a sufficient distance within this line to allow for the thickness of strip and hinges. When the screen is set up with the panels at angles to each other, of course the matching line is violated, but this effect is minimized if the panels match when the screen is fully extended (all panels in the same plane).

Dummies

In every case—photomural, overmantel, or screen—a scale dummy should be made for study purposes. I make up about 6 proof prints 16x20, and use them to determine the final trim of the panel or panels, etc. If possible, I prepare a small working dummy, cut in 3 or 4 panels if a screen is to be made, so that I can see how the screen will look in various positions. Likewise, if a multiple-panel mural is to be made I prepare a dummy, and see how the trimming lines will relate to forms and lines in the subject. It often takes a lot of time and experimentation to decide how to trim each panel so that the image will not lose its compositional effectiveness and yet to keep panels the same size. Trimming on or near a vertical line in the subject is obviously to be avoided.

43. Screen: Orchard in Winter. This screen was made from a 6x9 section of an 8x10 negative. It was enlarged in 3 sections. Each panel is 6 feet high, mounted on ½-inch plywood and framed in aluminum channel strips. The effect of the screen is somewhat softer than it appears in this reproduction; a large screen or photomural of small-print brilliancy would be overpowering as an element of decoration.

The client will appreciate a more inclusive scale dummy of the screen, over-mantel, or mural project, showing its placement in relation to the structure in which it will be installed.

In closing, I beg to remind the reader that murals, overmantels, and screens are very expensive to do well—and are very bad indeed if done poorly. But a whole new field is open to the serious photographer who wishes to investigate the possibilities of using photography in decoration. I have not discussed using photographs as wallpaper, mounted under glass (or imbedded in plastics) for table tops and trays, or applied to fabrics. Space does not allow such discussion, but the interested photographer can use his imagination and abilities in expanding his art in many new directions.

Detailed Procedures

We will presume that a dummy has been prepared and the panel, or panels, are carefully planned as to size, proportion, and matching edges. We will also assume that the laboratory is equipped with a precise enlarging apparatus, a fine enlarging lens (I use an 18-inch Zeiss Apo-Tessar), and an adequate easel panel. We will also need adequate processing trays, washing sinks, and drying frames. I use three stainless-steel trays—about 50 inches long (55 inches would be better if the use of 50-inch wide paper is contemplated), 12 inches wide, and 9 inches deep. I use the standard 40-inch rolls of *double-weight* bromide or chlorobromide papers—preferably in 10-yard lengths. (Rolls can be especially ordered in almost any practical length.) Single-weight paper is usually advised, but I am of the strong personal opinion that double-weight paper offers more advantages; it is sturdy, and easier to process.

For a developer I use a modified Ansco 130 (see page 114). Development must be long, as it takes some little time to roll and unroll the long paper sheet in the solution. I plan for 6 minutes' development. If matched panels are being made, I use a separate 10-liter bath for each 40x72 sheet. The proper amount of restrainer is added according to the test instructions on page 60.

I use an acid stopbath of standard formula in the second tray, in which I place the print (constantly rolling and unrolling it (see Fig. 44) for several minutes. In the third tray I have the usual acid hardener fixing bath. After immersing it in this bath I roll and unroll the print constantly for about 3 or 4 minutes, then place it face up in my large washing sink (about 5x7 feet by 1 foot deep). I spray off the surface and store the print in it until the second fixing takes place. I can also examine the print in its entirety, and match it to other prints if necessary.

The technique for immersing the dry roll in the developer solution is as follows: The print is loosely rolled as it is taken off the easel panel. It is placed in the developer with the loose end on the bottom of the tray and toward the operator (Fig. 44 a). This end is pulled toward the operator and rolled loosely, as in Figure 44 b; smoothness of movement is aided by unrolling the other end at the same time. When the new rolling is completed (Fig. 44 c), the process is reversed. It takes a little practice to achieve this rolling process without undue delay. The image will appear with alarming lack of uniformity; streaks and blotches and empty areas will always startle the operator; but if the rolling and unrolling of the paper has been carried out steadily and without too much delay, the print will soon assume a consistent tonality. Within about 4 minutes the image should be entirely even throughout. Development should be complete in from 5 to 6 minutes, but an additional minute or so will assure thorough processing. (In making panels to be matched in tone, the development time must *always* be the same—and with the same amount of fresh developer at the same temperature —and, as far as possible, with the same tempo of rolling and unrolling the sheet.)

When development is complete, make the last roll somewhat tighter than the others, place both hands under the roll and *slowly* and *gently* lift the roll out of the solution, tipping it so that the solution within the roll will drain out slowly. A sudden lifting of the roll from the solution may result in serious damage; the solution in quantity is heavy, and may break the roll. When the roll is out of the developer, and free from most of the solution (this can be judged from the weight of the roll), it can be tipped sharply and drained for say 15 seconds, then placed in the stop bath. It should be unrolled in the stop bath without delay, and the treatment should be continuous. The roll is lifted from the stop bath with the same care as from the developer, and placed in the fixing bath. It is lifted from this with equal care and placed in the water. We must always remember that large prints are prone to bending, breaking, and pinching when moved rapidly or forcefully in solutions; all movements must be *slow* and *gentle*.

When all the panels are made, they are separately rolled up and stood on end to drain. *One at a time,* each is put through the second fixing bath for 4 or 5 minutes, replaced in the washing sink, face up, and hosed off with a gentle spray. (A third fixing can be given if desired; if so, the time in each fixing bath should be slightly reduced.) When fixing is complete, the water in the washing sink can be changed a few times in rapid succession, removing most of the fixing solution from the prints. (The prints must be kept separated and in continual motion.) Then the prints should be washed for *at least* 3 hours, with constant agitation, and with frequent complete draining of the wash water. This additional washing time is for safety; with large print surfaces the water may not reach the center of the print readily. When the washing time is up, the prints should be separately rolled up and stood on end to drain. The wash water is drained, and then one print is replaced in fresh water and washed for 10 or 15 minutes. It should be turned over several times (by rolling, lifting out, replacing the other side down, and unrolling), and both back and front should be gently hosed off with a gentle spray. It

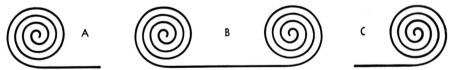

44. Schematic Diagram: Cross Section of a Large Print Being Processed. The print (3 to 10 feet long) is rolled up when taken from the easel, placed in the developer, and rolled from one end to the other as shown. If the motion is steady and continuous, a minimum of inequalities will appear in the first few minutes of development; on completion of development the print should show no unevenness of tone (see text, pages 108-09).

is then rolled up, taken gently from the water, and stacked on end to drain. The next print is treated likewise, and so on until the entire set is thoroughly processed. With an important assignment, I have found it economical to make 2 identical prints of each section; the possible loss by accident in processing and mounting must not be overlooked.

Large screens of light wood or metal frames and stretched cheesecloth or light sheeting are good for drying large sheets of paper. I distrust the method of drying large prints by hanging them up; I have had them warp out of shape by their own weight. Lay the prints face up and swab off excess moisture, then roll, place face down on the screens, and swab off excess moisture from the backs. When placing the prints on the drying screens, have the screen nearly horizontal; but when ready to dry, the screen can be tilted to about 45°, and the frames, if suitably separated one from the other, can be stacked in this position. Of course elaborate drying devices can be designed and made, but the above method works splendidly.

When the prints are dry, pile one on top of the other and roll loosely, tying with two or three strings to keep the rolls firm, and stack on end for safekeeping. Do not allow the rolls to lie flat, especially on uneven surfaces.

Details

Be especially careful for darkroom fog; the exposures are usually long.

Be sure the safelights are really safe.

Do not turn on any other lights until you are sure the unexposed paper is securely put away. Paper in such quantities is *expensive*!

A 1½-inch pipe, or a round wooden shaft about 50 inches long, can be attached on one side to the top of the easel panel by a sturdy hinge, and the paper roll can be slipped on it. The shaft is then swung back and latched into a support on the other side of the easel. The paper can then be pulled down like a window blind and secured by thumbtacks. (Begin securing at the bottom and work up either side, being sure to take up any obvious bulge in the paper.) When the paper is fully secured, with a sharp knife trim the sheet off just under the roll. Put final thumbtacks along the top, remove the roll from the support, place it in the box, close the box, and proceed with the exposure. After exposure, remove the thumbtacks from the bottom first, rolling up the sheet as the tacks are removed. Remember that paper absorbs moisture; if the darkroom is humid, the paper may acquire moisture from the air and buckle during exposure. Hence the darkroom must be as dry as possible.

A large glass door-panel could be used to press the paper firmly in the flat position, but such an installation would be expensive and heavy, and would favor the production of dust spots. An elaborate suction device can be made to hold the paper against the easel. If the easel is surfaced with a thin sheet of iron, magnets (such as Alnico) can be used to support the paper; this is a rapid and efficient system.

Focusing will be a real problem. The images of great enlargements are usually faint. A focusing magnifier is essential. I make focus tests by exposing small pieces of fast paper and noting the sharpness of the negative grain. When the negative grain is sharp, we have achieved maximum precision of focus; often the image itself is not sufficiently sharp to determine even an approximate focus. Remember that the lens-to-negative distance is critical, the lens-to-paper distance not so critical. Any bulge in the negative may throw off the enlarged image to a damaging extent. Hence the use of glass negative carriers is advised.

For the smoothest effects I use diffused light for murals. This implies a fairly long exposure—up to 5 minutes or more. Reciprocity departure of the paper is bound to occur; I therefore usually use a somewhat vigorous developer, and I often employ a grade more contrasty paper than would be used for regular prints from the same subjects. All such problems can be resolved by tests such as will be found on pages 12 and 62. The use of collimated illumination, while usually requiring much less exposure, will reveal and exaggerate grain and physical defects in the negative to an alarming degree. I feel that a mercury-argon tube grid, used with high voltage, will provide the most efficient and satisfactory illumination. A Photoflood lamp placed back of the tubes can be used for focusing, and turned off when the enlargement is made. Dodging, burning, and edge-burning are done as with ordinary enlargements, but of course these expressive controls must be very exact if sequential panels require them. Rehearse position and timing before applying to an actual enlargement.

In making a multiple-panel mural or screen, the ideal system is to have a large enough easel panel to permit projection of the entire image. Strips of paper are then placed on the different parts of the image, with sufficient overlap—say at least 1 inch on either side. Of course the strips are placed and exposed one at a time. In darkrooms with insufficient space for projection of the entire image, the negative carrier of the enlarger can be designed to raise and lower the negative and move it sideways—thereby bringing various parts of the image into the field. If the apparatus is precise and the lens of the finest quality, free from distortion of any appreciable kind, this method is entirely satisfactory. With my equipment I can match 6-foot prints within $\frac{1}{8}$ inch in allover length.

Some Professional Aspects

We do not sell photomurals and screens as we do simple prints or moderate enlargements. I am completely opposed to anyone's buying a photomural "out of stock." The possibilities of such a mural's being appropriate to its environment in color, scale, surface, and—not the least important—subject matter is quite remote. A photomural or a screen should be *planned* for its specific setting; the client should be urged to understand that such an installation is really a type of major interior decoration, and out of fairness to all, it should be carefully considered. A well-done photomural or screen is expensive, and a poorly done one is worthless. The following points should always be discussed with the client:

1. *Subject.* The client may first favor some literal landscape or still-life arrangement. Impress upon him that he might soon tire of a literal photographic treatment of a literal subject. Discuss the advantages of simple patterns from nature—patterns not dissimilar to tapestry effects, or to semi-abstract compositions. Show the advantages of vigorous compositions for areas of high circulation, and of quiet compositions for continuous "living with."

2. *Scale.* Sheer size is not important; the scale and proportions should relate to the wall space, the height of room, and the viewing distance.

3. *Definition and technical perfection.* Especially if the murals are to be viewed close at hand, the definition and the finish should be precise and clean.

4. *Tone and surface.* Needless to say, the tone should relate to the environment. The values should be somewhat softer than those of small prints. The surface should be adjusted to minimize possible reflections from windows and lights.

5. *Construction.* Of the finest quality; permanent prints, mounted to avoid warp, and firmly attached to the wall surfaces, with appropriate trim.

FORMULAS

STANDARD DEVELOPERS

These developers are listed in the PHOTO-LAB-INDEX, but are put in tabular form here for convenience and for comparison purposes. Be certain to read the "remarks" before mixing. Refer to the PHOTO-LAB-INDEX for further data. A Kodak developer is designed to work primarily with Kodak papers, etc., but most developers will work with most papers (see page 12 for testing procedure). Formulas marked * are available in prepared form.

As time goes on, more and more proprietary formulas are produced; for example, Dektol, Vividol, Selectol, Selectol-Soft, etc. These are high-quality products. Selectol-Soft can be used in discrete combination with Dektol as an alternate to the Beers formulas.

Mix ingredients in sequence from left to right except when figures in ( ) indicate otherwise. Do not add any ingredient until the preceding one is thoroughly dissolved. Use only pure water for solutions (preferably distilled). A 10% solution is made by mixing 1 unit of solid in 9 units of water; when dissolved, add water to make 10 units. For example, 10 grams Potassium Bromide dissolved in 90 cc water, then add water to 100 cc. A 10% solution is easier to measure than a very small amount of dry chemical.

FORMULA NUMBER	INSTRUCTIONS FOR USE	Water to Mix (125° F)	Metol (Elon, Verriol)	Sodium Sulfite, Desiccated	Hydroquinone	Sodium Carbonate, Desiccated OR	Sodium Carbonate, Monohydrated	Glycin	Amidol	Potassium Bromide, 10%	Water to Make
		cc	g	g	g	g	g	g	g	cc	cc
ANSCO *103	Dilute 1 part stock solution with 2 parts water. Further dilution gives soft results. Used full strength, this developer gives quite contrasty results.	750.0	3.5	45.0	11.5	67.0	78.0			12.0	1000.0
113	Use full strength for the most brilliant effects. Dilutions up to 1:20 give progressively softer effects with good tone. Give ample developing time with high dilutions.	750.0		44.0					6.6	5.5	1000.0
120	A soft-working developer, giving good print color. Sometimes used with 103 or 125 (in sequence) for contrast control of prints. For use, dilute 1:2 or more. Can be used full strength.	750.0	12.3	36.0		30.0	36.0			18.0	1000.0
*125	A standard developer. For use, dilute 1:2, for softer results, 1:4. This formula gives considerable flexibility of contrast with varying exposure and development times.	750.0	3.0	44.0	12.0	55.0	65.0			20.0	1000.0
130	A brilliant, cool-toned developer. Use solution full strength for maximum contrast. Normal dilution 1:1. For soft effects dilute 1:2 or more. See page 114 for my personal variation of this formula.	750.0	2.2 (1)	50.0 (2)	11.0 (3)	67.0 (4)	78.0 (4)	11.0 (6)		55.0 (5)	1000.0

Code	Description								
135	A rich, warm-toned developer. Use 1:1 dilution. For soft effects dilute up to 1:4. Adding potassium bromide increases warmth. Adding benzotriazole (antifoggant) will make the print cooler in tone.	750.0	1.6	24.0	6.6	20.0	24.0	28.0	1000.0
DuPONT 51-D	A warm-toned developer. For normal use dilute 1:1.	750.0	1.5	22.5	6.3	15.0	17.5	15.0	1000.0
*53-D	All-purpose developer (can also be used for films). For normal use dilute the stock solution 1:2.	500.0	3.0	45.0	12.0	67.5	79.0	19.0	1000.0
*54-D	For blue-black tones on most papers. Suitable for commercial finishing, etc. Dilute the stock solution for normal use.	500.0	2.7	40.0	10.6	75.0	88.0	8.0	1000.0
*55-D	For warm tones on most papers. Addition of potassium bromide will increase warmth of tone. Dilute the stock solution 1:2 for normal use.	500.0	2.5	37.5	10.0	37.5	43.9	40.0 to 130.0	1000.0
56-D	A fast developer for papers, giving somewhat cold tones.	500.0	3.3	33.5	10.0	56.0	65.0	33.0	1000.0
KODAK *D-52	Portrait-paper developer, gives fairly warm tones that are increased by the further addition of potassium bromide. For use, dilute 1:1.	500.0	1.5	22.5	6.3	15.0	17.5	15.0	1000.0
*D-72	A universal paper and negative developer, giving a tone of rather cold blue-black quality. Dilute 1:1 to 1:4 for various papers. Further dilution and addition of potassium bromide increase warmth of tone. See PHOTO-LAB-INDEX, Page 6-63.	500.0	3.1	45.0	12.0	67.5	88.0	19.0	1000.0

Not only are some formulas available in prepared form (those above marked *), but some manufacturers provide special proprietary developers (Selectol, Vividol, etc.) that are entirely satisfactory, stable, and economical. These developers, in the main, are designed to give rather warm tones.

The above listed developers are **standard.** It has been my experience, however, that as the photographer progresses in craft and esthetic sensitivity he will demand a greater amount of control than is easily achieved through the standard developers. The formulas that follow below have certain advantages which the reader should investigate for himself.

MY PERSONAL VARIATION OF THE ANSCO 130 DEVELOPER

I mix as specified above, **excepting** that I omit the hydroquinone and the restrainer and reduce the sodium sulfite to 35.0 grams. The Metol-glycin combination gives a very fine neutral tone. I add the antifoggant as required to the working solution (see page 61 for fog test). If more contrast is desired I add as needed the following hydroquinone solution:

Water	750.0 cc
Sodium Sulfite, desiccated	25.0 grams
Hydroquinone	10.0 grams
Water to make	1000.0 cc

BEERS TWO-SOLUTION FORMULA (From Jordan and Wall, **Photographic Facts and Formulas,** courtesy American Photographic Publishing Company, Boston.)

To me, this is one of the most useful of all formulas, in that a wide range of contrast control is possible. The original formula calls for potassium carbonate, but I use sodium carbonate with complete success.

SOLUTION A		SOLUTION B	
Water	750.0 cc	Water	750.0 cc
Metol (Elon)	8.0 grams	Hydroquinone	8.0 grams
Sodium Sulfite, desiccated	23.0 grams	Sodium Sulfite, desiccated	23.0 grams
Sodium Carbonate, desiccated	20.0 grams	Sodium Carbonate, desiccated	27.0 grams
or monohydrated	23.4 grams	or monohydrated	31.5 grams
Potassium Bromide 10% sol.	11.0 cc	Potassium Bromide 10% sol.	22.0 cc
Water to make	1000.0 cc	Water to make	1000.0 cc

These stock solutions are mixed in the following proportions to give a progressive range of contrasts. The lower-numbered solutions can be further diluted for very soft effects.

CONTRAST	LOW		NORMAL				HIGH
SOLUTION NO.	1	2	3	4	5	6	7
A	8	7	6	5	4	3	2
B	0	1	2	3	4	5	14
Water	8	8	8	8	8	8	0
Total ounces	16	16	16	16	16	16	16

My personal variation of this formula is to mix the above with the exception of the potassium bromide, then to add the restrainer (potassium bromide or antifoggant) as required for the paper and the effect desired. (Refer to page 18 for description of the effect of the restrainer.)

EDWARD WESTON'S AMIDOL FORMULA

Water	800.0 cc
Sodium Sulfite, desiccated	35.0 grams
Amidol	11.0 grams
Potassium Bromide	7.5 grams
BB Compound (antifoggant; stock solution)	60.0 cc
Water to make	1200.0 cc

The addition of a small amount of citric acid (5 to 10 grams) acts as a preservative. It may slow the action of the developer a little, but not seriously.

WARM-TONE GLYCIN DEVELOPER (Edwal 106)

Water	750.0 cc
Sodium Sulfite, desiccated	85.0 grams
Sodium Carbonate, monohydrated	170.0 grams
or desiccated	145.0 grams
Glycin	28.0 grams
Hydroquinone	9.0 grams
Potassium Bromide	4.0 grams
Potassium Bromide 10% sol.	40.0 cc
Water to make	1000.0 cc

Dilute with 7 to 15 parts of water, the latter dilution giving '"engraving-brown" effects.

STOP BATH

Acetic Acid 28%	48.0 cc
Water to make	1000.0 cc

To make 28% acetic acid, dilute 3 parts glacial acetic acid with 8 parts water. Glacial acetic acid is dangerous to skin and the respiratory tract. Do not breathe the fumes or allow it to splatter on skin.

FIXING BATHS

The standard fixing baths may be found in the PHOTO-LAB-INDEX. Only the Kodak F-5 is given here:

	1 liter	4 liters	1 gallon
Water	600.0 cc	2400.0 cc	80 ounces
Sodium Thiosulfate (hypo)	240.0 grams	960.0 grams	32 ounces
Sodium Sulfite, desiccated	15.0 grams	60.0 grams	2 ounces
Acetic Acid 28%	48.0 cc	192.0 cc	6 ounces
Boric Acid, crystals	7.5 grams	30.0 grams	1 ounce
Potassium Alum	15.0 grams	60.0 grams	2 ounces
Water to make	1000.0 cc	4000.0 cc	1 gallon

This can be easily memorized: The proportion of hypo is 2 pounds to the gallon, with 2 ounces each sodium sulfite and potassium alum per gallon, 1 ounce boric acid, and 6 ounces acetic acid 28%. **Always mix the ingredients in sequence as listed above.** If the acid is added before the sodium sulfite, the solution will precipitate.

NONHARDENING METABISULFITE FIXING BATH

It is claimed that this fixing bath gives better print color, but it should not be used when solutions or wash water exceed 70° F, or when the Kodak HE-1 (Hypo Eliminator) is to be used.

Water	
Sodium Thiosulfate (hypo)	800.0 cc
Allow to cool; then add	475.0 grams
Potassium or Sodium Metabisulfite	67.5 grams
Water to make	1000.0 cc

PLAIN HYPO FIXING BATH

	1 liter	4 liters	1 gallon
Water 125° F	800.0 cc	3200.0 cc	80 ounces
Sodium Thiosulfate (hypo)	240.0 grams	960.0 grams	32 ounces
Water to make	1000.0 cc	4000.0 cc	1 gallon (128 oz.)

See page 54 for description of use.

HYPO TEST SOLUTION (Kodak HT-la)

Refer to PHOTO-LAB-INDEX, Section 6, p. 101, for full description. This is a much better formula than the ordinary potassium-permanganate solution.

GOLD-PROTECTIVE SOLUTION (Kodak GP-1)

This is a valuable formula; not only does it assure permanancy of the print, but it also can be used to "cool" the tone should the tone be too warm from action of the developer, or too warmly toned.

Water	750.0 cc
Gold Chloride (1% stock sol.)	10.0 cc
Sodium Thiocyanate or	
Potassium Thiocyanate	10.0 grams
Water to make	1000.0 cc

Prepare a 1% stock solution by dissolving 1 tube (1 gram) in 100 cc of water. Add the gold-chloride solution to the 750.0 cc water. Dissolve the sodium thiocyanate **separately** in 125.0 cc water. Then add the latter to the gold-chloride solution while stirring the latter solution rapidly. Immerse the fully washed print (or the print treated with the HE-1 solution) for about 10 or more minutes. Watch for a perceptible change of image tone; it will gradually become slightly bluish-black. Then wash thoroughly for about 10 minutes, swab, rinse, and dry as usual. Approximate life: 30 prints 8x10 per gallon. The solution should be mixed immediately before use for the best results.

WETTING AGENT

I recommend Kodak Photo-Flo. Use as directed. There is no doubt that surface water will drain faster from prints treated with this compound. The addition of a wetting agent to the developer is of questionable advantage.

TONING FORMULAS

Numerous toning baths are formulated in the **Photo-Lab-Index,** in **Photographic Facts and Formulas,** (Wall and Jordan) and in many general textbooks. I use the selenium toner for general work. In previous editions of this book I gave the formula for preparation of this toner from the basic chemicals. However, since selenium is a quite poisonous substance in its "metallic" state it is best to obtain it in the relatively safe liquid form, such as the prepared Kodak Selenium Toner. It is important to use a fresh fixing bath (and a 2nd and 3rd plain hypo bath following the first bath) and, after washing, to immerse the prints in a 2% Kodalk solution prior to toning. This will prevent stained whites and prolong the life of the toning bath. I have found that the time of immersion in the 2% Kodalk bath is not critical, providing it is at least 10 seconds with good agitation. I dilute the stock toning solution with 10 to 12 parts of water, and tone at a moderately warm temperature (75°F). This yields rich, cool blacks on Velour Black, Kodabromide, and similar papers. For papers such as Opal or Cykora I dilute the toner with 3 or 4 parts of water, achieving a quite warm tone. However, in terms of conventional standards of toning, selenium works only on chloride or chloro-bromide papers. My personal concept of "tone" is more a "cooling-off" of the greenish cast so obvious in many modern papers, the production of a cool-purple-sepia tone in very slight degree, and the enrichment of the deeper tones of the image. For strong tones, the Hypo-Alum process, the Nelson Gold Toner, and the regular bleach-and-redevelopment sulfide toners are suggested. For a detailed description of toning with selenium refer to page 78.

The recently introduced hypo-eliminator solutions (see page 55) used with added selenium toning solution gives excellent results and considerably shortens total processing time. I use 200cc Kodak Selenium toner per gallon of hypo-eliminator solution, and bathe the prints therein (constantly agitated) for 5 to 15 minutes, depending on the degree of toning desired. The fixing baths must be **fresh,** a second bath is strongly advised. From the first fresh bath, prints can go to water storage; then just before putting in the hypo-eliminator-toning solution, they can go through the 2nd hypo bath. Kodak advises taking the print directly from the fixing bath to the hypo-eliminator-toning bath to avoid stains but this shortens the life of the bath, due to the acid fixing bath carried into it. The procedure of regular fixing bath, followed by water rinse (or storage), then a fresh **plain** hypo bath, followed by the hypo-eliminator-toning bath and washing has worked well for me with hundreds of prints. Use a blue "daylight" light to judge toning and make comparisons with a wet untoned print.

REDUCTION

General reduction of the print can be effected by a short immersion in Farmer's Reducer (Book 2) diluted 1:3 or more. To avoid the possible stain, even after prolonged washing, the iodine-cyanide print reducer described in **Photographic Facts and Formulas** (Wall and Jordan) is advised. Local reduction in iodine-thiocarbamide (again see **Photographic Facts and Formulas**) is quite practical. The following formula is designed to serve as a slight bleach, providing a means of clearing the whites and brightening the image to a very considerable extent.

A	Water	300.0 cc
	Potassium Ferricyanide	62.5 grams
	Potassium Metabisulfite or	
	Sodium Bisulfite	4.2 grams
	Water to make	500.0 cc
B	Water	600.0 cc
	Ammonium Thiocyanate	330.0 grams
	Potassium Bromide	30.0 grams
	Water to make	1000.0 cc

Take 1 part of A and 2 parts of B and 10 to 15 parts of water. Immerse the dry print face up with vigorous agitation for 5 to 10 seconds. Place immediately in water and agitate until the bleaching solution is assumed to have been removed from the surface of the print. Examine; return if necessary to the bleaching bath (advised only for a few seconds). If the print is wet, or if the solution is too dilute, the middle and lower tones may respond to the action of the bleach thereby weakening the print values in general.

PRINT INTENSIFIERS

Selenium toning slightly intensifies prints. Using the intensifiers designed for negatives (in dilutions of 3:5) will give the prints more "body," but may have serious effects on the print quality and color.

116

CONTRAST CONTROL

The water-bath process, so favorable to the negative (see Book 2) can to a certain extent be applied to the print. I find that the best developer is Amidol—any one of the formulas listed here is adequate—and the treatment is somewhat the same as for the negative. Develop until all the important values (below Zone VII grays) are visible, then put the print in a tray of still water (without agitation), and watch for the growth of the lighter values. Within a minute or so, the maximum effect in the water bath is gained, and the print should be returned to the developer for a short immersion—say 20 seconds—then back to the water. The object is to achieve solid black, but also the proper gradations of the high values. Mere physical relationships—such as are acceptable in the negative—will not suffice in the print, for the print is truly seen (looked at), and the basic values must be securely established.

Another process, known as the "Sterry process" (listed in **Photographic Facts and Formulas**), is very effective, but usually when print color is not judged to be important. After exposure and before development, the print is immersed in the following bath:

STOCK SOLUTION

Potassium Bichromate	3.7 grams
Ammonia	1.0 cc
Water	85.0 cc

Take 10 ounces water and add to it 20 to 50 minims of stock for chloride papers, 50 to 100 minims for bromide papers, or an intermediate amount for chloride papers. The amount used is subject to trial with various papers. Put the print in this working solution for 2 or 3 minutes; then rinse in running water for several minutes, and develop as usual. Trial is important; too prolonged treatment in this solution will impair print color.

RESTRAINERS

The common restrainer is potassium bromide. I advise using it in a 10% solution. Benzotriazole (Kodak Anti-Fog #1) is excellent, and has many advantages over potassium bromide in that it gives a pleasing color—on the cool side. It should be diluted for use according to the manufacturers directions.

P.O.P. TONING AND FIXING BATHS

There are quite a number of toning and fixing baths published today—although they are a meager residual of the formulas that were in practical use in earlier days. I have found that the following formula will work satisfactorily with most P.O.P. available today:

A	Boiling water	500.0 cc
	Hypo (Sodium Thiosulfate)	125.0 grams
	Potassium Alum	7.5 grams
	Lead Acetate	1.0 grams
	Water to make	600.0 cc

Dissolve the hypo and the alum, let the solution cool, filter it, and add the lead acetate dissolved in a little distilled water.

B	Distilled water	100.0 cc
	Gold chloride	1.0 grams

To use, add 6 cc of B to 100 cc of A and let the mixture stand for 24 hours. Print for degraded highlights, then, in a very subdued light, wash the prints until the wash water ceases to look milky. Then immerse the print in the toner. Toning must be continued for not less than 10 minutes. Use a **very** clean tray—porcelain or glass—and keep temperature at about 65° F.

STAIN REMOVERS

Refer to the PHOTO-LAB-INDEX, and to other works, for a variety of stain-removal formulas and tray cleaners. A simple tray cleaner is:

KODAK TC-1	Water	750.0 cc
	Potassium Bichromate	90.0 grams
	Sulfuric Acid C.P.	96.0 cc

Add the sulfuric acid **slowly** while stirring the solution rapidly. Pour a small amount of the solution in the tray or container, rinse around so that it contacts all parts, then pour the solution out and rinse **thoroughly**.

SPOTTING COLORS

Apart from the dye-spotting colors, the regular pigment or ink-base color has many advantages. Edward Weston kindly permits me to give his formula: Use equal parts (by weight) of Chinese (stick) ink and gum arabic; dissolve in enough water to cover these ingredients, and mix. Let dry out and mold to suit. Moisten a brush in water (to which a wetting agent may be added), wipe on a piece of paper until the proper gray shows, then apply to the print. A "dry" brush works much better than a "wet" brush. The amount of gum arabic may be increased 2 or 3 times to increase the sheen of the spotted area on the print.

PRINT VARNISH

Proprietary varnishes are entirely adequate. The prime requisites are purity of ingredients and good color—rather, lack of color when applied to the prints. Paul Strand has kindly given me his formula for surfacing prints (in his own words): "First, one buys a small can of lithographer's varnish No. 1. . . . This should last for years. Next one buys a bottle of Carbona (carbon tetrachloride), the solvent for the varnish. . . . A good way to get the varnish into the Carbona is with a swab stick, letting it run off drop by drop until the Carbona is a lemon-yellow color after shaking. The varnish is then ready to apply with a piece of cotton. Cover the print thoroughly . . . then smooth the whole surface out by taking almost all the varnish off by rubbing briskly with a piece of dry absorbent cotton. . . . The varnish is slow-drying (3 or 4 days) . . . and I have never noticed any evidence of discoloration." This print varnish is for matte, semimatte, and semigloss prints.

TRANSPARENT LACQUERS (for spraying on prints)

There are a number of suitable materials on the market. I advise consulting with the DuPont Corporation for detailed specifications. Kodak Print Lacquer is perhaps the best material available. Spraying is much faster than hand application, and a far more satisfactory means of applying such substances to the prints. New products are always appearing on the market; I hesitate to make any positive recommendations here.

PERCENTAGE SOLUTIONS

1% solution: dissolve 1 gram in 90 cc water; then add water to make 100 cc. 10% solution: dissolve 10 grams in 90 cc water; then add water to make 100 cc. Refer to the PHOTO-LAB-INDEX, Section 12, p. 10, **A Simple Formula for Diluting Solutions.**

STRETCHING OF PHOTOGRAPHIC PAPERS WHEN WET

There is a considerable increase of size of any standard photo paper when wet, especially in the direction of the paper grain. After washing and drying the paper returns to approximately its original size. But when large prints are moistened and mounted with paste, a definite swelling is observed and is only slightly reduced when dry. But the contractive force remains, and will cause warping and bending of the mount unless it is very rigid, or if a piece of similar paper is mounted on the back. For precise evaluations of swelling of any paper, consult the manufacturer.

INDEX

A

Acetic acid, 53
  glacial, 3ln.
Adams, Ansel, books by, 3, 97
Adamson, Robert. *See* Hill, D. O.
Agitation, 52
Amidol, 49-51
  Developer (Weston's), formula, 114
Ansco 130 Developer, 112
  Adams' variation, 114
Antifoggants, 47-49, 61
Arizona, photos, 30, 77
Atget, Eugene, book by, 3
Autumn, Glacier National Park, photo, 59

B

Beers Two-Solution Developer, formula, 114
Books on photography, list, 3
Boric acid, 53
Boulder Dam, Calif., photo, 38
Brady, Mathew, ref. to, 4
Brilliancy, 19, 25, 96-97
  enhancing, 58
  limitations of, 19
Buildings, photos, 11, 16, 51-53, 69, 81, 90, 95, 98

C

California, photos, 16, 20, 38, 48, 51, 66, 81, 95, 98, 102
Callier effect, 21-22, 104
Calotypes, 2
Carbon process, 2
Carbro process, 2-3
Church, San Francisco, photo, 51
Clearing print whites, 56
Clerc, L. P., book by, 2n.
Collodion process, 2
Collotypes, 95-96
Colonial Doorway, photo, 44
Contrast, 7, 46; photo, 48
  control, 117
Curves, paper, 14
  developing, diagrams, 15
  symbolic, diagrams, 7, 10

D

Daguerreotypes, 2
Darkroom, 27-44
  accessories, 61
  lighting, 27-29
  precautions, 29-31, 61
  preparing the, 60-61, 78, 99-100
Defects, 30-32, 34, 36-39, 43, 52-56, 76, 78, 88 91-94, 110
Densitometers, 22, 43, 58
Developers, 45-46, 60-61
  for mass production, 103
  formulas, 112-18
  ingredients of, 46-52
  temperature of, 50
Development, 45-46
  effect of, on print image, 14-21
  rule for, 21
  static, photo, 53
  water-bath, 49, 61; photos, 48, 53
Dixon, Maynard, photo, 77
Dodging, 66-71; photos, 68-69
  symbols, 70
Doorways, photos, viii, 44
Draining, 55-56
Driffield. *See* Hurter and Driffield
Drying, 56
  toned prints, 79-80
Dudley, Beverly. *See* Henney, Keith

E

Easel, enlarging, 34, 37-39; diagram, 35
Eastman Kodak Company, 42

E

Edge-burning, 66; photos, 66, 68-69, 71
  equipment, 67-71 (illus.)
  symbols, 70
Emerson, P. H., book by, 3
Enlargements, 21-22
  equipment for, 34-43 (diagram)
  focusing for, 39-40, 73-74
  lenses for, 36, 74
  lighting for, 34-36, 40-43 (diagram), 73-74
  making (detailed description), 73-75
  optical and technical considerations, 75-76
  possible troubles, 74-75
  tests, 74, 76
Enlargers, 22, 33-43, 73-74; diagram, 35
Etching prints, 91
Exposure
  judging, 62
  rule for, 21
  scales, 9-10
  tests for effective, 10-13, 17-18, 64-65
Expressive print, the, 1

F

Farm, Mount Diablo Range, Calif., photo, 16
Fixing baths, 53-55, 61, 103
  formulas, 115; P.O.P., 117
Flare, camera and lens, 36
Focusing
  for enlargements, 39-40, 73-74, 110
  magnifier, 39, 73, 110
Fog, 16-18, 29, 36, 39, 45, 47, 55-56, 60-61, 64n., 65, 76, 110
  tests for, 12, 74
Formulas, 112-18

G

Gas Station, Richmond, Calif., photo, 95
Glacier National Park, photo in, 59
Glycin, 50
  Developer (Warm-tone), formula, 114
Gold Protective Solution, formula, 115
Golden Gate Bridge, photo, 66
Grand Canyon, The, Ariz., photo, 30
Grand Teton, The, Snake River, photo, frontispiece
Gum process, 3

H

Half Dome, Winter, Yosemite, photo, 72
Halftones, 95-97
Head of a Nisei Girl, Manzanar, Calif., photo, 20
Henney, Keith, and Dudley, Beverly, book by, 4n.
Hill, D. O., and Adamson, Robert, book by, 3
Hoover Dam, Calif., photo, 38
Hurter and Driffield, quoted, iv.
Hydroquinone, 46-47, 50
Hypo, 53-54
  Eliminator, formula, 115
  Test Solution, formula, 115

I

Illumination. *See* Light; Lighting.
Intensifiers, 116

J

Jordan, Franklin I. *See* Wall, Edward J.

L

Lacquer, 91-94, 118
Lantern slides, 5, 19
Leaf Pattern, photos, 33
Lenses for enlargements, 36, 74
Lester, Henry M., books by, 3
Light
  diffuse, 22, 40-43 (diagram)
  collimated, 22, 42-43
  viewing, 19-21, 29

119

Lighting for
  darkrooms, 27-29
  enlargements, 34-36, 40-43 (diagram), 73-74
  photomurals, 110-11
  printing, 42
  toning, 78
Lithographs, 95-96

M

Mass production, 99-103
Mesa Verde National Park, photo in, 90
Metol, 46-47, 50
Metronome, 35, 62
Morgan, Willard D., books by, 3
Mountains, photo, frontispiece, 71
Mounting, 28n., 83-89; photo, 85
  dry, 79, 84, 86-88 (diagram); press, diagram, 89
  photomurals, 105-06
  toned prints, 79-80
  varnished prints, 94

N

Negatives
  reading, 23-24
  relating to paper, 21-22
Nevada Fall, Yosemite, photo, 26
New Church, Taos Pueblo, N. M., photo. 11
Newhall, Beaumont, book by, 2n.
New Jersey, photos, viii, 44
New Mexico, photo, 11
Newton's rings, 32, 34
New York City, photos, 52-53, 69

O

Old Doorway, N. J., photo, viii
Orchard in Winter (photo screen), photo, 107
Overdevelopment, 16
Overmantels. *See* Photomurals.
Ozobrome process, 2-3

P

Palladiotype process, 3
Papers, 4-8
  bromide, 5, 14-16 (diagram), 57, 79
  bromochloride, *see* chlorobromide
  chloride, 14-15 (diagram), 57, 79
  chlorobromide, 5, 14, 16, 57, 79
  contact-printing, 5
  developing-out, 3, 5
  grades, 9, 23
  printing-out, 4
  properties of, 9-25
  relating negatives to, 21-22
  selecting, 1, 6-8
Percentage solutions, formula, 118
Perspective, 75
Photo screens, 106-07 (photo)
Photograms, 4
Photogravures, 95-96
Photo-Lab-Index, ref. to, 36, 39, 52 (photo), 58, 80, 112-13, 115-18
Photometers, 22, 43, 74
Photomurals, 75, 104-11
  diagram of processing, 109
  dummies for, 107-108
Plastics, 1, 94
Platinotype process, 3
P.O.P. Toning and Fixing Bath, formula, 117
Potassium alum, 53
Potassium bromide, 47
Portraits, photos, 20, 63, 77, 102
Pressing, 56-57
Priest at Mariposa, Calif., photo, 102
Print color, 6, 24-25, 46, 49-50, 104
Printing
  boxes, 32-33
  contact, photo, 33; equipment for, 31-33 (diagram), 60
  frame, 31-33
  processes (historical), 2-3
Prints
  development, effect of on image, 14-21
  expressive, 1
  making (detailed description), 60-73; for reproduction, 95-97
  mass production, 99-103
  processing, 45-58
  surfacing, 94

R

Reciprocity departure, 42, 46, 62, 76, 110-11
Records, importance of keeping, 25
Reducer, formula, 116
Reduction potential, 49n.
Reflection density. *See* Brilliance.
Reproduction, making prints for, 95-97
Restrainers, 60-61, 65, 117
  test for, 18, 60-61
Rocks, photos, 26, 30, 38, 59, 82
Rotogravures, 95-96

S

Safelights, 27-29, 61
San Francisco Residence, photo, 81
Selenium Toner, formula, 116
Sierra Nevada, photo, 82
Sludge, 31
Snow, photos, 72, 107
Sodium carbonate, 47
Sodium sulfite, 46-47, 49n., 53
Sodium thiosulfate, 54
Spotting, 91-94
  colors for, 117
  toned prints, 80
Stain Remover, formula, 118
Step wedges, 10-13, 18, 58
Stieglitz, Alfred, 1, 5, 92, 96
  books by, 3, 96
Stop baths, 53, 61
  for mass production, 103
  formula, 115
Strand, Paul, 1, 25
  book by, 3
  varnish formula by, 91, 118
Stretching of photographic papers, 118
Sunlight on Old Boards, photo, vi
Swabbing, 55-56

T

Tests for
  enlargements, 74, 76
  exposure, 10-13, 17-18, 64-65; photo, 63
  restrainer, 18, 60-61
Timers, 35, 62
Tioga Lake, photo, 71
Toners, 79-80
Toning, 57-58
  detailed description, 78-80
  formulas, 116; P.O.P., 117
  lighting for, 78
  mass-production prints, 103
  split, 57-58
Transparencies, 5, 19
Trees, photo, 72

V

Varigam, 5, 8
Variography, 39
Varnish, 1, 25, 92-94
  formula, 91, 118

W

Wall, Edward J., and Jordan, F. L., quoted, 116-17
Warm-Tone Glycin Developer, formula, 114
Washing, 55
  toned prints, 79-80
Watch Tower, The, Mesa Verde National Park, photo, 90
Water, photos, frontispiece, 26, 71
Waxing, 1, 25, 94
Weston, Edward, 1, 5, 84
  book by, 3
  formulas: Amidol, 114; spotting, 92, 118
Weston Analyzer, 10, 22-23, 43, 58
Weston Step Wedge, 10-13 (illus.), 76
Wet-plate process, 2
Wetting agent, 116
White Church, The, Hornitos, Calif., photo, 98
Winery Interior, Lodi, Calif., photo, 48
Wood, photos, vi, 82, 98
Wood and Rock, Noon Sun, Sierra Nevada, photo, 82

Y

Yosemite, photos, 26, 72

120